Young **Men** *on the* **Margins**

Anne Cleary

Maria Corbett

Miriam Galvin

Joy Wall

Commissioned and Published by
The Katharine Howard Foundation

ii

The Katharine Howard Foundation
ISFC
10 Grattan Crescent
Inchicore
Dublin 8

Tel. 01 453 1861
Fax 01 453 1862
khf@eircom.net

First published by The Katharine Howard Foundation.

Printed and designed by Genprint Ireland Ltd.

ISBN 0-9546911-0-5

This study forms part of The Katharine Howard Foundation's publications series in which it is No. 2.

Contents

Foreword

Minister of Social and Family Affairs, Ms Mary Coughlan T.D.

I welcome this important report 'Young Men on the Margins' which was completed under this Government's Family Research Programme.

The Families Research Programme was developed to support research projects, which have the ability to inform the future development of social policy and to address the issues that face our society today.

This report highlights a number of family-related risk features that were evident in the study of homeless men. There were identifiable routes to homelessness and the trajectory started at a very early age, usually within the family unit. It shows the effects of a lack of support at crucial stages in the lives of the young men interviewed, and the excluding effect of poverty and the difficulty of breaking out of the cycle of disadvantage.

Poor levels of education, followed by little or no vocational training, a lack of success in the job market and a background of personal, familial and health difficulties appear to be common features. What is evident is that the increasing isolation and alienation of a particular grouping of men who are in this situation is due to a combination of structural, familial and personal factors.

This excellent piece of research will inform the effective targeting of resources to where they are needed and this is a key feature of this Government's social policy agenda.

We are very pleased to have assisted the production of this report on a valuable research project initiated by The Katharine Howard Foundation into the circumstances of young men on the margins of society.

I would like to thank The Katharine Howard Foundation for this excellent piece of research and in particular Anne Cleary and her team for their hard work in completing this study. I look forward to the publication of further quality research studies under the Families Research Programme, which is now the responsibility of the Family Support Agency.

Ms Mary Coughlan TD
Minister for Social and Family Affairs

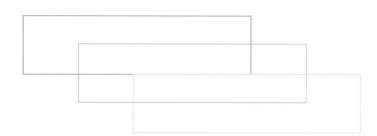

Authors' Acknowledgements

The authors would like to thank the Social Science Research Centre, National University of Ireland Dublin (NUID), in particular Pauline Faughnan and Máire Nic Ghiolla Phádraig who facilitated the project in many ways. Thanks are also due to Máiríde Woods who read the initial draft of the report and provided advice and additional material.

A number of individuals and bodies were generous with information. These included Paul Corcoran and Helen Keeley (National Suicide Research Foundation), Benny Swinburne (Department of Social and Family Affairs, previously Department of Social, Community and Family Affairs), Brendan Doody (Child Psychiatric Services, South Western Area Health Board), Selina McCoy (Economic/Social and Research Institute), Ros Moran and Mary O'Brien (Health Research Board), Paula McKay and Ian Daly (South Western Area Health Board) and P.J. McGowan and Kieran O'Dwyer (Garda Síochána).

Along with The Katharine Howard Foundation we would like to thank the research team who assisted in completing the work. Thanks are due to the members of the Advisory Group, Fergus Carpenter, Joe Kelly, Brendan Walker and Heber McMahon who gave generously of their time to the project and to Kieran McKeown, Mel Cousins and Tony McCashin who assisted in the early stages. This research was partly funded through the Families Research Programme in the Department of Social and Family Affairs and we would like to thank the Minister, Ms Mary Coughlan and the staff of the Family Affairs Unit in the Department for their

4

support. We would also like to acknowledge the Family Support Agency, now responsible for the Families Research Programme, who have kindly assisted with the publication costs.

Special thanks are due to Clare Farrell whose editorial skills helped bring the report to increasing levels of comprehension and to Joan O'Flynn for her editorial assistance with the final edit.

All those involved in this research project would like to recognize the assistance provided by the men who agreed to be interviewed for the study. They were willing to give their time and relate, sometimes painful, experiences to help us. We hope this document is an honest portrayal of their lives and words. Contact with these men would not have been possible without the kind facilitation shown to the researchers by the staff and management of the centre attended by the men and for that we are extremely grateful.

Anne Cleary,
Department of Sociology,
National University of Ireland Dublin

January 2004

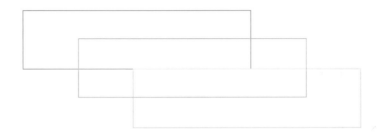

An Introduction
by The Katharine Howard Foundation

The Katharine Howard Foundation, as an independent grant making body, places a particular emphasis on supporting projects and initiatives in disadvantaged communities. In the course of its involvement in supporting community groups throughout Ireland in recent years, the Foundation has become aware of considerable numbers of men, mostly young men, who have little or no participation in family life, community life, or employment. Typically they have benefited little from the education system, are unskilled and unemployed. Some are fathers, and some not. Increasing numbers, living in both urban and rural areas, are becoming socially excluded. There is growing concern about the numbers of such men addicted to alcohol or drugs, involved in crime, becoming homeless or resorting to suicide.

Although there is no shortage of opinions about the reasons for this, careful enquiry by the Foundation indicated that very little serious research seemed to have been done to identify the origins and the processes that lead to men finding themselves in this situation. The Foundation believes that research into why particular social problems arise, the impact they have on individuals and communities, and how they might be overcome or prevented in the first place, can provide invaluable material to help policy makers target and respond to social need. With this in mind the Foundation, assisted by an Advisory Group, sought proposals from researchers, aimed at discovering how such men become marginalized. The sub-title of our brief to researchers was "Unskilled, uneducated, unemployed and socially excluded men – what went wrong? – present help and future prevention". The work

6

was carried out in the Social Science Research Centre at University College Dublin, with Anne Cleary as Project Director. The research was completed by Anne Cleary, assisted by Maria Corbett, Miriam Galvin and Joy Wall.

In the last few years, there were a number of efforts and initiatives to meet some of these men's needs through Centres for the Unemployed, Local Employment Services, and the Department of Social and Family Affairs (previously the Department of Social, Community and Family Affairs) Grants for Locally Based Men's Groups. These have met with some success. Many of the initiatives have aimed at intervening in difficult situations, often when marginalisation has already occurred. It is the Foundation's belief that, if possible, it is best to identify the causes, and provide early interventions which interrupt cycles of disadvantage and the process of marginalisation. Successfully doing this produces a better result for the individual, the community, the State and the country's economy.

Having discussed a number of different approaches to the research work, it was decided initially to undertake a qualitative study involving in-depth interviews with twenty homeless young men in Dublin City. At the same time a review of available data and existing research outlining how boys and men fare within the family, the community, the education system, and the work-place was undertaken. A study of attempted suicide among young men was also done, and it is intended to publish this separately at a later date.

This report examines the issue of homelessness among young men, in the context of wider issues raised by the literature review and the assembly of data on marginalisation among men in contemporary Ireland. It is presented in three sections.

❖ The first section gathers together existing material from a wide variety of sources and provides a context and a backdrop.

- ❖ The middle section is based on the in-depth interviews which enable the homeless young men to tell their stories. The Foundation believes the most important source of information in a study such as this is the experience of the individuals themselves, as told by them.
- ❖ The final section reflects on how the experiences of the men in the case study relate to the broader contextual picture outlined in the first section, and attempts to draw out some lessons from the findings.

Overall the report provides an invaluable insight into the lives of a group of men we rarely get to hear from directly, and some understanding of how and why some men end up homeless. It highlights:

- ❖ The way in which, from childhood onwards, difficult experiences in the family, the education system, and the wider community cumulatively impact on and disadvantage individuals, particularly when there is little or no support at an early stage.
- ❖ The lack of support at crucial stages later on in the lives of the young men interviewed.
- ❖ The excluding effect of poverty and the difficulty of breaking out of the cycle of disadvantage.
- ❖ The articulated desire on the part of many of the men to change their lives and become integrated into society – even when this seems extremely difficult.

The Foundation believes that the report makes a valuable contribution to a better understanding of how some men become alienated from their families and their communities, and the cluster of factors which, when coinciding in a human being's life, lead to feelings of worthlessness and failure. The contextual analysis of a great deal of data and other documentary sources will in itself provide a valuable resource for students, researchers and policy makers.

The Katharine Howard Foundation also believes that the men's stories underline the need for the continued development of a wide range of community based preventative and support programmes for children, families and communities. Close integration of agencies providing these services will strengthen the outcomes. The extent and influence of socio-economic disadvantage on the men's lives and their pathways to homelessness suggests that the social costs of a divided society are too great.

Issues that arise from this, and other research on disadvantage and marginalisation, include:

- ❖ The need for a great deal more support (trained and dedicated personnel, not simply money) for parents who are having difficulty coping with the challenge of parenting.
- ❖ The need to intervene at the earliest opportunity to nurture children, particularly those at risk of social exclusion, through early childhood care, development and education.
- ❖ The need for more extensive school based interventions such as psychological and learning support.
- ❖ The need for gender-specific education and preparation for life in both the formal and informal education spheres.
- ❖ The need to support boys or men who are already "on the outside" to develop the resources, skills and confidence to actively change their lives.
- ❖ The need for continued investment in effective drugs prevention and rehabilitation services.
- ❖ The need to explore the development and expansion of youth diversion programmes.
- ❖ The need to focus on housing and homeless services with a greater sense of urgency.

In relation to these, The Katharine Howard Foundation asks three key questions worthy of considered debate and attention. Are all these issues purely the responsibility of the State and semi-State sector? Are there any lessons to be learned from work being done and services being provided in other countries? Finally, are the rights of boys and men receiving the attention they deserve?

In the broader social policy context, continued commitment to the Government's National Anti-Poverty Strategy is important particularly now that the growth of the economy has slowed. The National Children's Strategy also provides a valuable framework within which the strategies and services to interrupt cycles of disadvantage, and improve the well-being of Irish children, can be developed in a focused and co-ordinated way.

We would like to express our thanks to the many people who supported this work. The research was co-funded by various statutory and private sector partners, including The Allen Lane Foundation, The St. Stephen's Green Trust, an anonymous donor, the Department of Social and Family Affairs (previously the Department of Social, Community and Family Affairs) and the Family Support Agency. The support and encouragement offered by all our co-funders in undertaking this research is acknowledged with gratitude.

The Advisory Group, whose experience and wise counsel has been invaluable, and to whom we are greatly indebted, consisted of Fergus Carpenter, Joe Kelly, Brendan Walker and Heber McMahon, with Kieran McKeown, Mel Cousins, and Tony McCashin giving assistance in the early stages. Noreen Kearney and Philip Jacob represented The Katharine Howard Foundation and gave very generously of their time and assistance throughout the process of this research.

The Katharine Howard Foundation owes a particular debt of gratitude to its Development Officer, Noelle Spring, who had overall responsibility for managing this research project from its commission to its completion. Despite a busy workload in other areas of the Foundation's work, Noelle's focus and commitment to this project was unstinting, and is very much appreciated.

This report has focused on one particular group of marginalised men, but it has taken this focus in the context of an overview of the nature of men's marginalisation. This report will soon be complemented by another on the issue of suicide. The research raises questions for further study and discussion, and we hope that the publication of this report opens up a space for this investigation and discussion to continue.

The Katharine Howard Foundation
January 2004

Executive Summary

The so called 'crisis of masculinity' is based primarily on diverse research findings and anecdotal evidence. The main aim of this report is to investigate the reliability of these claims by examining the evidence for marginalisation in key areas of consequence for men and to explore the experience and background to marginalisation through the stories of a number of men from a socially excluded group.

Methodology

For the qualitative study, in-depth interviews were conducted with twenty men aged 18-30 years who were attending a drop-in centre for homeless men in Dublin. The interviews were semi-structured and were tape-recorded. Data for the contextual analysis was gathered from documentary and other sources.

The Context of Male Marginalisation

The Family

❖ Family changes, including an increase in lone female parenting, have challenged traditional values around marital and sexual relationships. People have, in general, adjusted to these developments and some men have welcomed the opportunity to refocus on fatherhood and home issues. Yet family change may have benefited fathers within rather than fathers outside the home. Marriage may now be less available to some young men for economic reasons and because of the greater likelihood that a woman will set up home, with her child, on her own.

❖ The absence of a father may result in negative social and psychological outcomes for males but this is dependent on his access to alternative sources of affirmation and models of behaviour, the parenting ability of the remaining adult and economic resources. It is also dependent on the child's relationship with the out-of-home father.

Education

❖ The comparative academic attainment levels of girls and boys in Ireland have reversed in just over two decades. Girls are now outperforming boys at all educational levels (with the exception of higher level honour grades and postgraduate qualifications). Yet, gender and socio-economic grouping interact quite significantly in terms of educational performance. Not all males are equally affected and boys from better off backgrounds perform significantly better than boys from lower socio-economic groupings.

❖ The educational difficulties encountered by some males may originate in early problems experienced in home and school environments. Boys are more likely to have specific learning and or literacy difficulties. It is also more probable that they will externalise problems, all of which make progression through school problematic without early remedial assistance. Expectations around traditional male roles and behaviour are also likely to push less successful students into environments which are more realistic for them in terms of identity and self-affirmation.

Work

❖ The decline of traditional male work areas, alongside the rise of job sectors accessible to both men and women, have transformed the labour market in Ireland and elsewhere. There is still strong adherence amongst men, especially working class men, to traditional work areas despite their potential vulnerability in a recession.

❖ Poverty and disadvantage can give rise to marginalisation for men in a number of ways. Poor school outcomes are closely linked to economic vulnerability in the marketplace and this trajectory is more common amongst males than females. Men from lower socio-economic backgrounds do significantly less well in the job market than men from higher socio-economic backgrounds. Economic factors, especially unemployment influence the ability to set up an independent home and also affect access to marriage or long term relationships and fatherhood.

Marginalised Lifestyles

❖ Certain similar features can be identified in different marginalised groups, in particular the homeless, those who abuse drugs and offenders. These are predominantly male categories. Poor levels of education, followed by little or no vocational training, followed by lack of success in the job market and a background of personal, familial and health difficulties are common elements. The similarity of characteristics apparent in the various marginalized categories point to similar pathways to exclusion.

❖ The increase in crime over the past three decades in Ireland may be related to the economic exclusion of working class male groupings. Young, working-class men, especially those from disadvantaged backgrounds are over-represented among offenders and crime is also associated with specific geographical, disadvantaged locations. Drug use is closely linked to crime and both drug users and offenders tend to come from similar, disadvantaged backgrounds.

Changing Value Systems and Psychological Marginalisation

❖ Attitudes to religious and moral issues have changed substantially in Ireland in the last two decades. Young people especially demonstrate more of the liberal values associated with a secular, individualist society but there is no evidence of extreme individualism nor isolation.

❖ There is greater acceptance of suicide and this is especially so among young males who are the category most likely to complete suicide. Individuals who take their own lives are influenced by more widespread acceptance of suicide and lessening religious ties. Work and family change may also impact negatively on men's lives especially in the context of men's lack of confiding relationships and difficulties in disclosing distress. Economic factors are important in that men appear to be more affected psychologically (than females) by their relatively poor position in the economy. Those who attempt or complete suicide are more likely to have low levels of educational and work skills and marginalised groupings, such as the homeless and offenders, are particularly at risk of suicide.

The Experience of Marginalisation

❖ The conclusion of the qualitative study of homeless men is that the cause of homelessness for these men is connected to structural issues of poverty, to the effectiveness and level of the educational resources they received, to their ability to avail of these services, to personal issues embedded in their family experiences and to gender factors.

❖ What emerges from the men's narratives is that a series of difficulties in their young lives – personal, familial, educational and structural – narrowed their life options as they grew to adulthood. They were overwhelmingly from economically deprived backgrounds. Their early family lives were characterised by multiple traumas especially loss, disruption and instability. Many had experienced the absence of parenting, either because a parent had left the family home, or was unable to cope. These men lacked role models. Relationships with their fathers were often conflictual and they did not have substitute figures outside the family.

❖ The participants had a very low level of educational qualifications. Their experiences of school were generally ones of exclusion and they began to disengage early in second level. The lack of educational skills was both cause and effect of developing allegiances to out of school interests and activities. Leaving home was usually precipitated by difficult or abusive home situations or because they had become involved in drug-taking. Once out of home these men, unable to survive in the labour and housing markets and vulnerable to negative economic and personal events, slid into homelessness. Exiting from this state became increasingly difficult as their problems were compounded by the out-of-home life. They were also becoming increasingly isolated socially. Some participants maintained contact with families but those from splintered families avoided isolation only by developing friendships and support within the homeless system. These attempts were not generally sucessful and many of the men were demoralised and psychologically marginalized.

Conclusions

Even though there is widespread change in masculine roles the evidence is that many, perhaps most, men are adjusting and adapting to change. Some categories of men, mainly young, working class men, have found these social and economic transformations difficult. Males from these backgrounds are more likely to lack the economic and wider social benefits of education and marriage. Fatherhood may now be less of an option for them than in the past. These features are exemplified in the lives of the homeless men studied. They were also at risk of psychological marginalisation in that loneliness and despair was affecting their mental health.

The conclusion of this report is that despite challenge and confusion amongst men there is no general crisis of masculinity.

16

There is evidence, however, of the increasing isolation and alienation of a particular grouping of men who are in this situation due to a combination of structural, familial and personal factors.

Introduction

Men, particularly young men, are experiencing difficulties in today's society. Indications of these difficulties can be found in the predominance of males in marginalised groups, such as the homeless, in the greater number of behavioural problems experienced by young men and in the suicide statistics in Ireland and other western countries. What has become termed 'the crisis of masculinity' is linked to a variety of factors: from the effects of social and economic change to more specific developments such as changing roles and expectations for men and an increase in drug and alcohol abuse. The decreasing importance of institutions such as organised religion and the family has also been implicated as a cause of new uncertainties in young lives, particularly those of men (MacInnes 1998; Harris 1995; Farrell 1994; Kimmel 1987). This report is an attempt to examine these issues in an Irish context. The report has two key aims:

❖ To explore and gain an insight into the experiences of a group of particularly marginalised young men in Ireland through an in-depth qualitative approach. This method allows us to listen directly to the voices of homeless young men describing their experiences.

❖ To draw together some available data on the experience of marginalisation among men and boys in contemporary Irish society in order to document and provide a wider context for understanding the qualitative material.

The context of the report is set by drawing on available data on boys' and men's possible exclusion. This offers a basis for understanding the qualitative study itself. The contextual section examines the areas of the family, work, education, marginalized subgroups, changing value systems and psychological alienation.

The main part of the report presents the findings of a qualitative study of homeless young men attending a drop-in centre for the homeless in Dublin. Here, twenty men talk directly about their lives. In particular they highlight experiences in childhood, in the family, in school and in the wider community, which influenced their path to homelessness.

In the final section of the report an attempt is made to examine how the experiences of the men in the qualitative study relate to the overall context set out earlier in the report. The aim here is to contribute to debates about homelessness and wider issues relating to the experience of marginalisation among men.

The Context of Maginalisation Among Young Men in Ireland

This part of the report reviews and documents information relating to marginalisation among young men in Ireland. From an initial documentary search a number of topics were identified as potentially important. These include the family, education, work and economic life, homelessness, substance abuse, crime, and changing societal values. The objective in the following sections is to provide an overview of how men and boys fare in these areas and to explore the connections between them.

1.1 Family and Changing Family Structures

This section traces changes in the Irish family over the last three decades and examines the contemporary nature of family life in this country. An attempt is made to isolate those factors which impact particularly on young boys and men.

There has been quite considerable family change in Ireland over the last three decades. Marriage is still overwhelmingly the option for couples setting up a home together but the marriage rate has fallen and diverse family forms are now common (CSO). Marital separation has also increased (Fahey and Russell 2001). Types of family units now in evidence include couples without children and lone parent families, the majority of which are headed by separated and never married females. After almost continuous decline since the 1970s, there was a slight upturn and then stabilisation in the national birth rate since the mid-nineties. The average number of children per family has declined (from 2.2 in 1981 to 1.8 in 1996) although Irish family size is still high by European standards.

Lone parent family units have increased considerably since the 1980s. Between 1988 and 1997 there was a 119% increase in the numbers of non-marital births and in 2000 approximately 32% of all births took place outside of marriage (Swinburne 1999; Fahey and Russell 2001). Fahey and Russell (2001) estimate that lone parent families make up approximately 14% of families with children under fifteen years. There is debate however about the relative importance of non-marital births vis-a-vis marital dissolution as the main reason for lone parenthood. The two family groups are almost exclusively (99%) female but have different age profiles in that separated parents are somewhat older than never married parents (Swinburne 1999; Fahey and Russell 2001). There is evidence of economic and other vulnerabilities amongst lone parent families in that these units are largely dependent on the State (Swinburne 1999). Swinburne's (1999) data indicate that lone parents receive little economic support from the father of the child although this may be an underestimate (Fahey and Russell 2001). Lone mothers are also more likely to have lower levels of educational and vocational skills than other mothers and are drawn disproportionately from lower socio-economic groupings (McCashin 1996; Fahey and Russell 2001).

Further changes impacting on the family since the 1970s include the greater propensity of married women to work outside the home and the consequent range of alternative childcare arrangements. The majority of Irish families are still headed by a male breadwinner but there appears to be increasing flexibility around parenting duties (McKeown, Ferguson and Rooney 2000).

The consequences of family change

The family environment, it is generally agreed, is key to later outcomes for the child. Children and young people need certain basic elements although there is flexibility about how, where and by whom they are delivered (Hill and Tisdall 1997). Available findings regarding the effect of differing family types on children suggest that the nature of the household is not the important factor but rather the quality of the relationships and the economic resources available to the family (Hobcraft and Kiernan 2001).

Despite a contemporary focus on lone parenthood, this family formation is not a new phenomenon although it is now more likely to be due to separation and non-marital births rather then parental death as in the past (Fahey and Russell 2001). Neither is there anything original about discourses of anxiety in relation to lone female parenting and absent fathers (Haywood and Mac an Ghaill 2003). There is a view that lone female parenting is detrimental to children, yet making generalisations about lone parents or single mothers (in Ireland) in the absence of comprehensive information is difficult as the social, economic and personal resources available to lone mothers vary greatly (Flanagan 2001; Fahey and Russell 2001). There is evidence that children in lone parent families are vulnerable to educational and or behavioural problems when the family is economically disadvantaged (Fitzgerald and Jeffers 1994; McMunn et al. 2001). Lone parent families tend to have fewer economic resources than families generally (Allen 1999). Early lone motherhood is a particular risk factor as it is associated with both economic and educational disadvantage in the mother (McMunn et al. 2001). In Fitzgerald and Jeffers' study (1994) children from single parent families were more vulnerable to developing disorder but only in conjunction with economic disadvantage. Kolvin, Miller, Scott, Gatzanie and Fleeting (1990) longitudinal study demonstrated how improvements in the family's economic situation benefited the child across a number of intellectual indicators.

There are risk factors for children within the home. Family discord and disruption are potentially problematic for all children but this is largely due to the type of problem involved and the resources available to the family and to the child (Rutter 1989; Carroll 2002). Family conflict which involves violence is a significant predictor of psychological ill-health for children (Kessler and McGee 1993). This underlines the main risk factor in relation to family discord i.e. when the child is directly involved in the conflict (Rutter et al. 1998). Similarly, parental psychiatric disorder, especially in the mother, has been identified as a vulnerability factor for children as it adversely affects the mother's ability to parent the child (Fitzgerald and Jeffers 1994).

In general children emerge from childhood as psychologically healthy because they are resilient, adaptive and can access protective elements in their environment (Garmezy 1987; Gilligan 1993; Horwitz et al. 2001). For example there is no evidence that children have been affected by the large-scale movement from home care to other forms of childcare which has occurred in Ireland over the last twenty years (Hennessy 2001). Even with the most severe adversities, it is unusual for more than half of all children affected to succumb to a maladaptive outcome (Rutter 1979). In fact successful negotiation of difficult environments can have a positive impact on the child's development (Beardslee and Poderefsky 1988). Thus the effect of parental psychiatric illness is lessened if only one parent is affected and the remaining parent is able to compensate. Secure attachments and good quality parent-child relationships in early childhood serve as major protective factors (Grotberg 1995). The occurrence of multiple difficulties appears to be key in relation to outcomes for children (Lazarus and Folkman 1984; Rutter and Quinton 1977). A single negative element may have little effect on the child but multiple deprivations, co-existing in the same family will have more profound effects (Kolvin et al. 1990).

There are gender differences in response to family and other difficulties and this is evident from a young age. Males are more vulnerable when there is family discord and boys are more likely than girls to develop emotional and behavioural difficulties in these circumstances (Rutter 1987). Boys are more likely to react to problematic family situations in an aggressive way and this is likely to elicit negative reactions from parents (Maccobe and Jacklin's 1974). However there is evidence that parents are more likely to argue in front of sons than daughters and for boys to be the target of parental hostility, neglect and abuse (Hethering, Cox and Cox 1982; Rutter 1987; Nygaard Christoffersen 2000). Young boys are also less likely to disclose problems and or to seek help (Lawlor and James 2000). Yet the visible manifestations of young male distress are more likely to attract the attention of parents and teachers and result in referral to social and medical services. The impact of behavioural difficulties on the mother in particular may prompt her to seek help. Findings from the child psychiatric services support this in that referrals to the Dublin services are predominantly male and are referred at a younger age than girls. Over three-quarters of the male presentations had developed problems before or during primary school (in contrast to 55% of the girls) and 18% (in contrast to .05% of the girls) were first referred to the service at the pre-school stage (Doody 2000).

Young boys are more likely than girls to develop externalising disorders such as behavioural and conduct problems (Rutter, Giller and Hagell 1998). Young girls' distress tends to be internalised and displayed in less obvious and thus more 'socially acceptable' ways (Cleary 1997b). It is possible therefore that both males and females are affected equally by family and other problems, but the effects of such problems on girls may lie dormant or at least hidden for longer (Cleary 1997a). However, early behavioural disturbance has been cited as among the strongest predictors of later problems (Rutter 1989; Kolvin et al. 1990). Conduct difficulties make it more likely that there will be an early exit from school with the resulting employment difficulties (Fergusson and Horwood 1998). There is

24

also a greater risk of the child becoming involved in substance abuse and juvenile offending (Fergusson and Lynskey 1998). Although behavioural and conduct disorders are common in childhood they do not, in general, persist into adulthood (Rutter 1989). The risk of continuation is greatest when there is a combination of factors such as aggression and a specific learning difficulty (Loeber 1990). And if these problems persist they can become increasingly resistant to treatment (Sheerin, Maguire and Robinson 1999).

The documented increase in behavioural disorders over the last fifty years has been linked to changes in family formation (Rutter and Smyth 1995) although this association has been disputed (Furstenburg 1991). It is the possible relationship between the concurrent rise in male behavioural disorders and lone parent families which has excited the most debate. The evidence cited above indicates that single parenthood per se is not a vulnerability factor for male behavioural difficulties unless there are other and sufficient causation. Yet there is a strong political theme that associates 'troubled masculinities' with lone female parenting and the absence of a father figure (Hearn 1998). According to Clare (2000) boys need a male figure or role model to develop into psychologically healthy adults. He maintains that the sons of absent fathers have difficulties forming long-term relationships and are more likely to engage in anti-social behaviour. There is little doubt that the presence of a father is a very positive force in a child's life and that some children have little or no access to their biological father (Flanagan 2001). Yet the absence of a father is not inherently problematic for the male child. As with family difficulties generally, the impact of an absent father would be dependent on the child's ability to avail of substitute role models and sources of support as well as the child's experience of, and relationship with, the (absent) father. Indeed, as Haywood and Mac an Ghaill have said, absent father usually implies the absence of a 'good father' embodying notions of authority and economic responsibility (Haywood and Mac an Ghaill 2003, p.56). These debates give little recognition to the changing nature of fathers and fatherhood and the fact that there are now diverse models of fatherhood (Hochschild 1995). Consequently these discourses often pathologise men generally and working class men in particular (Haywood and Mac an Ghaill 2003). While in the past fatherhood had a limited set of meanings and possibilities for a man, in the context of the changing family and the fragility of non-marital relationships, the father-child bond may now be the most permanent relationship in a man's life (Beck and Beck-Gernsheim 2002).

Family changes resulting from women working outside the home have resulted in both positive and negative outcomes for men. There has been a refocusing on fatherhood and men, in general, are seeking closer relationships with their children (McKeown, Ferguson and Rooney 2000; Kiely 2001). Yet there has also been a lessening of links due to increasing marital separation as well as career demands (Hochschild 1995). Thus while middle class men now generally subscribe to the notion of the new father they are often prevented from developing this role because of work commitments.

The entry of married women into the labour market has affected marital relationships in other, significant, ways. There is some evidence that men have been affected by both the changing power balance and the reduced availability of spousal support (Stack 1998). Marriage is a positive environment for men (but less so for women) in that married men are more likely to be psychologically healthy than single men (Cleary 1997a). The better mental health status of married men is attributed to the higher levels of emotional and other support received. The affirmative basis to marriage for men is evidenced by the finding that a significant movement by married women into the workforce negatively impacts on men's mental health (Stack 1998). While the marriage state may be proving more challenging for those within the institution, the marital option may be less available to some men. The fact that lone parent family units are more numerous today and are, in general, headed by women indicates a willingness by young women to accept the responsibility of single parenthood (Katz, Buchanan and McCoy 2000). The initiation of a family unit has become a possible option for a young woman with a child even when there is no financial or other support from the father of the child. This option inevitably reduces the opportunities for some men to become part of a family of their own and this is especially so if they are economically disadvantaged. Unemployment is linked to diminution of marriage prospects among young men and a significant correlation has been found between lone parenthood and male unemployment (Webster 1997a). A similar pattern might well have developed in Ireland in the 1980s in the context of poor employment prospects for both single female and male parents "who in better circumstances might have become the husbands of the mothers in questions" (Fahey and Russell 2001, p.67). The fact that marriage and its emotional benefits may now be less accessible to young men implies a loss situation for them.

Summarising points

❖ There have been quite considerable family changes in Ireland over the last three decades and diverse family forms are now common. The number of lone parent families, headed by a separated or never married woman, has risen sharply since the 1980s. However, traditional family units still predominate and the majority of children are raised in two-parent families.

❖ The absence of a parent may be important in relation to certain outcomes, including behavioural difficulties, in the child but this is dependent on a number of factors. These include the child's access to alternative sources of affirmation and models of behaviour, the parenting ability of the sole or remaining adult and economic resources. When these features line up in a negative combination, especially in lone parent families with no adequate supports, the children may be vulnerable. Negative outcomes for children are usually only evident when there is reliance on only one source of parenting and when this parenting is inadequate in the context of economic disadvantage.

❖ The explanation for boys' greater tendency for overtly deviant behaviour as they develop may be explained in terms of a greater propensity amongst males to externalise problems from an early age. Boys and young men who experience behavioural difficulties are more likely to come to the attention of school and specialist services and are less likely to have successful school careers.

❖ Family changes have challenged traditional values around marital power relationships and childcare responsibilities. Marital and sexual relationships are more fluid and lack permanence. Yet these developments have not always resulted in negative outcomes. Irish children and their parents have, in general, adjusted to these developments and some men have welcomed the opportunity to refocus on fatherhood and home issues. It is possible however that the gain in terms of family change may have benefited women more than men. Marriage may have become less available to some young men and in the light of the positive effects of marriage for men this may represent a loss for them.

1.2 Educational Skills and Resources

In Ireland educational opportunities have increased significantly over the last three decades. Similar developments in other countries indicate that not all children have benefited equally (Phillips 1993). The following section examines gender and socio-economic differentials at each educational level and the employment implications of educational participation.

Educational participation and performance

There is, as yet, little available data relating to performance in primary education in Ireland although analysts widely regard this as the formative educational site (Department of Education and Science 2000). Recent findings indicate that individual needs and difficulties become apparent at a very early stage in the schooling process, and if these are unmet they will carry over into second level. In a study of Irish primary school pupils, boys overall were doing less well than girls (but only marginally so) across various educational parameters including cognitive and language development and reading ability (Hayes and Kernan 2001). Male pupils attending disadvantaged schools (as defined by Department of Education and Science) were doing particularly badly, scoring lower than all other groups (i.e. boys and girls from non-disadvantaged schools and girls from disadvantaged schools) on almost all measures. However boys from non-disadvantaged schools scored highest of all the groups on all measures (except, interestingly, perceived competence).

At second level, retention levels for males and females illustrate the fact that gender differentials, originating in primary school, begin to manifest themselves early on in the second level system. Increased retention levels are evident at second level in the Irish educational system from the 1980s. The percentage of those remaining until completion of the Leaving Certificate rose from 60% in 1980 to over 80% in 1998. Girls are more likely to successfully complete the educational cycle. Almost a quarter (24%) of male pupils exit before Leaving Certificate level compared to only 6% of girls and nearly two thirds (64%) of all students who leave without any formal qualifications are male (Economic and Social Research Institute 1998). Females are also more likely to outperform males in examination terms. Females attain higher aggregate grades than boys in all major public examinations (Clancy 1987; Lynch 1999) and they are more likely to take higher level papers in the Leaving Certificate Examination (National Council for Curriculum and Assessment 1999).

students to complete second level schooling and go on to university. Amongst pupils from working class backgrounds, females are more likely to complete Leaving Certificate but young males from lower socio-economic groupings are the least successful educationally. This group is also significantly over-represented amongst early school leavers. Boys and young men are performing less well educationally than females from all socio-economic groupings but there are significant differentials between males from professional and those from unskilled backgrounds. Thus, males may be underachieving in relation to females overall but not all males are equally affected. Young males from working class backgrounds emerge as a key risk group in terms of educational underachievement, a fact recognised by Irish education authorities (Irish Times 2003).

There is a substantial body of literature mapping the reasons why the school system may be incompatible with a child's class and gender background. Some analysts believe that educational regimes in general are too narrow and do not take account of the diversity of intelligences (Hanafin 2000). The educational system is viewed by others as dominated by middle-class frames of language and thinking and children from this background have an advantage (Bourdieu and Passeron 1977; Willis 1977). This can result in opposition and disengagement from school by the least successful working class students (Willis 1977; Connell 1989). Working class children are likely to have fewer education related resources available to them outside of school. There may also be greater dissonance between their home and school lives and parental expectations are also less likely to be framed in terms of further education for their children (Lynch 1999; Lareau 2000).

Students may also fail in, and disengage from, the system because they have difficulty learning. Learning and literacy difficulties are especially common amongst those who leave school early (Corridan 2002). In the UK a fifth of those who leave school early have a history of special educational needs compared with 2-3% of

32

all secondary school children (UK Audit Commission 1996 quoted in McGivney 1999, p. 28). Literacy problems are common in Ireland. It is estimated that a quarter of the population are functioning at a very low level of literacy skills and these difficulties are especially prevalent among boys and men (Morgan 1997). Poor basic skills in literacy and numeracy have overwhelming negative impact especially in relation to employment opportunities and other life chances (McGivney 1999). Learning and literacy difficulties increase the likelihood of educational failure as the young boy moves through the system. But they have more widespread consequences in that a lack of these skills limits one's competence in social interaction, emotional expression and communication generally. These deficits contribute to personal, social and economic isolation. This is supported by interviews with men with literacy difficulties who related experiences of exclusion and powerlessness from their schooldays (Corridan 2002).

Explanations for gender differentials within the educational system vary according to the level of schooling. In the primary system curriculum changes, with the emphasis on literacy and verbal skills, have been blamed. Girls, it is proposed, are more co-operative and have more positive attitudes to school. The predominance of female teachers has been cited as presenting problems for boys but this is not borne out by findings in Ireland or elsewhere. The fact that boys from non-disadvantaged schools were outperforming all other groupings at primary level in Hayes and Kernan's 2001 study refutes this argument. This finding also underlines the significance of economic and other, non-school, factors. Making additional resources available to disadvantaged schools does not necessarily result in equality of retention or performance although it will assist some pupils (especially girls). The family circumstances and socio-economic status of the child's family has emerged as key especially for pre-school and early primary school pupils (Kolvin et al. 1990). When disadvantage begins early in a child's life it may become established as a cycle of educational and other difficulties (Hannon and Ó Riain 1993;

Kolvin et al. 1990; Hayes and Kernan 2001). The reason (some) boys are doing less well at primary level may also be related to factors considered earlier in relation to boys' reactions to and manifestations of distress. Boys are more likely to externalise their difficulties and this will impact on the classroom situation. The foundations of second level performance are laid in primary school and some boys enter second level with too many risk factors for failure (Kolvin et al. 1990). For less able students this is likely to result in withdrawal from the system as studies of streaming show that as one moves down the educational system there is increasing disengagement from the school, especially for boys (Connell 1995).

There are issues for boys around traditional expectations of masculinity, especially working class masculinities, which affect school performance (Mac an Ghaill 1994). The school, as Mac an Ghaill has said, is strategically significant in shaping young men and masculinities. Strong pressures operate both within and outside the school to ensure young males adhere to traditional roles and expectations and schools offer interpretations of what it means to be a male or female (Lodge and Flynn 2001). According to Willis (1977) working class students actively resist the schooling process because it is not connected to real, manual, work. Similarly, Connell (1989) has spoken of one type of masculinity, which is formed by opposing the school authority structure while another category is created by smooth insertion into academic pathways. Those (and not merely working class pupils) who fail in the system may take up a range of alternative responses including adopting an 'exaggerated masculinity' (Connell 1989, p.67). Reliance on peer approval is usually strengthened as a source of identity affirmation in these circumstances. Some of these ideas resonate in studies of men who 'failed' in the education system (Owens 2000; Corridan 2002). In Corridan's (2002) study the men recounted concealing their feelings of alienation and displaying a strong masculine persona. Ignored and viewed as no-hopers within the system they expressed indifference to punishment, reworking their difficulties, in an attempt to control the situation, as 'going wild' or being a 'messer'. The emotional isolation which resulted from this ensured that their learning problems were not resolved and persisted into adulthood.

Summarising points

❖ The comparative academic attainment levels of girls and boys in Ireland have reversed in just over two decades and girls are now outnumbering and outperforming boys at all educational levels (with the exception of higher level honour grades and postgraduate qualifications). Females are more likely to complete second level schooling successfully and to go on to third level. At third level they dominate all sectors numerically and in the university system they dominate all subject areas including traditionally male subjects.

❖ It is apparent that gender and socio-economic grouping interact quite significantly. Boys may do less well educationally than girls in general but boys from better off backgrounds are performing well. Within the university sector gender is not related to completion and male students perform better in terms of higher level honours and higher degrees.

❖ Early school and family experiences provide the foundation for educational progress in later years and failure at this stage can seriously limit the life chances of children in a number of important ways. The difficulties encountered by some males may originate in early problems experienced in home and school environments. Boys are more likely to have specific learning and or literacy difficulties, which make progression through school, without early remedial assistance, problematic. If learning deficits are combined with behavioural disorders this will impact on classroom stability. These factors together make success at second level less likely.

❖ Expectations around traditional male roles and behaviour are likely to push less successful students out of the school system and into environments which are more realistic in terms of relevance and self affirmation.

❖ A particular grouping of male students can be identified as doing less well educationally. These are boys and young men from lower socio-economic backgrounds. Those in this grouping are performing less well at both primary and secondary level and are highly unlikely to enter the third level system. They are significantly over-represented amongst early school leavers and there are substantial educational differentials between them and females generally as well as males from the highest socio-economic groupings.

1.3 Work and Economic Marginalisation

Work has been described as key to male identity and to a man's status within his family and community, especially for working class men (Hearn 1998; Haywood and Mac an Ghaill 2003). This section examines trends in the Irish labour market and considers their possible impact on male roles and experiences. The links between economic and social marginalisation are also considered.

Male work patterns

Since the 1950s the profile of male work has changed considerably in Ireland (CSO various years). Up to the 1970s the Irish labour market was predominantly male-based. Since then the number of men in the labour force has grown but the level of male participation has not increased in line with their increase in the general population. Traditional male employment sectors (in particular agriculture and manufacturing) have also declined and male participation in these areas has decreased. Yet despite the constriction of these sectors, and the fact that these jobs tend to be relatively low-paid, unstable and low status in a high-tech economy, Irish males continue to enter these work areas

(Economic and Social Research Institute 1998). Male school leavers are over-represented in the agriculture, fisheries and industry sectors and over half of male school leavers (in contrast to a quarter of females) enter jobs in the industry sector. The disappearance of these 'masculine' work sectors is being replaced by a growth in the services sector, which is equally accessible for women and men. This, along with other developments has resulted in greater participation by women in the labour force.

Women's participation in the Irish labour market

Until the 1970s women's participation in the Irish labour force was largely confined to a limited number of occupations and a shorter period in the life cycle. While a man's working life generally spanned 40-50 years a woman's work life outside the home was usually restricted to 5-10 years. This was primarily due to the 'Marriage Bar' in the Irish Public Service, which up until 1973 obliged women workers in that sector to resign on marriage. There was also clear segregation by gender in that women workers were confined to a narrow range of occupations (in 1946, over 30,000 of the 37,000 women in the professions were in just three occupations: nursing, teaching or religious orders).

This pattern began to change from the 1970s on and between 1971 and 1996 the percentage of women in the labour force increased from 28% to 36% (Smyth 1997). The female labour force participation rate in Ireland is now 48.8% (CSO 2003). This increase in labour market participation has been especially marked among married women (Smyth 1997). Flexible working hours and conditions, alongside the development of work accessible to both men and women, have further facilitated this process of female labour market participation.

Economic status and resources

Despite an economic boom in the 1990s national studies have demonstrated the continuance of poverty among some groupings such as large families, lone parent households and the long-term unemployed (Callan et al. 1996; Whelan et al. 2003). Some children, especially those living in two parent families with a larger than average number of children, are especially vulnerable to poverty (Nolan and Farrell 1990). Economic disadvantage is concentrated in specific geographical districts and multiple deprivations are apparent in many of these areas (Gamma 1999).

Unemployment has decreased significantly since the 1980s (from 16% in the mid 1980s to an average of 3.9% for 2001). Similarly, long-term unemployment, a major contributor to poverty, declined steeply. However long-term unemployment continued among some groups (Fitzgerald et al. 2000). The long-term unemployed are predominantly male and those who remain unemployed in a buoyant economy are generally those with fewest educational and vocational skills, have health (or substance abuse) problems and perhaps a history of crime (Fitzgerald et al. 2000). Remuneration for the type of temporary, unskilled work available to these men often compares unfavourably with welfare payments and acts as a further disincentive to work (Fitzgerald et al. 2000). Over time they become disengaged from the labour market, thus increasing their marginalisation.

Implications for men
Economic disadvantage in families has implications for children in terms of education and other resources. This situation is exacerbated by the fact that poverty tends to cluster geographically alongside other forms of deprivation. Poverty and disadvantage, however, potentially affect both male and female children equally. Yet boys are more likely to become disengaged from school, particularly boys from economically deprived backgrounds. This phenomenon is related to differential reactions to, and expressions of, distress and to adherence to traditional masculine expectations and pathways.

The decline of traditional male work areas alongside the rise of job sectors accessible to both men and women has transformed the

38

labour market in Ireland and elsewhere. The well-charted routes for traditional masculinity are declining but yet young working class men still seek to follow these pathways. The adherence of some men to traditional work sectors increases their vulnerability in times of economic recession. This vulnerability is exemplified amongst the long-term unemployed. According to Haywood and Mac an Ghaill (2003) and McGivney (1999) the dilemma of working class men is that their sense of identity is bound up with traditional labour and they find it difficult to engage in different forms of employment. Women have experienced more positive economic developments over the past three decades. Married women especially have increasingly moved into the labour force since the 1970s and this has impacted on traditional relationships within the family with resulting gains for women and some men (as discussed in section 1.1).

There is a strong relationship between educational attainment and labour market success. Those exiting the educational system without qualifications are more likely than their qualified counterparts to be unemployed after leaving school (Department of Education and Science 2000; Economic and Social Research Institute 1998). Early school leavers also encounter greater difficulties in accessing further education and training opportunities and are far more vulnerable to unemployment. Thus despite significant improvements in employment opportunities for those with qualifications, those with no formal qualifications have fared less well (Clancy and Wall 2000). Boys from lower socio-economic categories are much more likely to drop out of school early and while both males and females have benefited from increased employment in the 1990s, the rapid growth of services in the labour market and the growing importance of this sector to the economy point to particular difficulties for young unemployed men with no qualifications or skills. Thus, although the overall proportions of young people experiencing unemployment one year after leaving school have fallen, the gap between the leaver whose father is unemployed and all other school leavers has remained constant. Socio-economic background also has a significant impact on school leavers' probability of continuing to further study after leaving school (Clancy and Wall 2000). This is particularly the case for leavers whose father is unemployed. Early school leavers are mainly male and from lower socio-economic backgrounds. This leaves them vulnerable to future unemployment in both the short and long term (National Economic and Social Forum 1997).

The reasons some men fall to the bottom of the economic ladder are both structural and personal. Education is decisively linked to employment. Employment, in turn, is a prerequisite to successfully establishing a separate household with marriage and children. This may prevent some men from ever developing a family unit (Webster 1997a). Those who do set up independent homes may remain in disadvantaged circumstances because their lower educational attainment and poor unemployment histories tend to maintain them in disadvantaged circumstances. Low educational attainment is therefore crucially linked to unemployment and may result in long-term and severe economic deprivation. Educational deficits (including literacy difficulties) are a feature of long-term unemployment. There may also be psychological implications. The association between unemployment disadvantage and mental well-being is well established in the literature (Nolan and Whelan 1997; Graham 2000) and there is evidence that economically disadvantaged males are more likely to be affected psychologically by personal disadvantage in a boom economy (Barber 2001). Young women from disadvantaged backgrounds, it may also be said, have a more 'socially acceptable' alternative to school and work in early motherhood (National Economic and Social Forum 1997).

Summarising points

❖ The decline of traditional male work areas alongside the rise of job sectors accessible to both men and women has transformed the labour market in Ireland and elsewhere. Yet there is still strong adherence amongst men, especially working class men, to traditional work areas despite their potential vulnerability in a recession.

❖ Despite economic boom, poverty is still evident amongst certain groups especially children in large and or lone parent family units and the long-term unemployed. Poverty and disadvantage can give rise to marginalisation for men in a number of ways. In conjunction with other difficulties in the home some children may be vulnerable especially in relation to school outcome. Poor school outcomes are closely linked to economic vulnerability in the marketplace and this trajectory is more common amongst males than females. Such males are over-represented amongst the long-term unemployed.

❖ Economic factors, especially unemployment, influence the ability to set up an independent home. They also affect access to marriage or long-term relationships and fatherhood.

❖ Economic disadvantage can affect the adult or child psychologically and the association between disadvantage and mental well-being is well established. There is also evidence that males are more likely to feel relatively deprived if economically disadvantaged in a boom economy.

1.4 Marginalised Lifestyles

Homelessness

Homelessness results from the convergence of a series of disadvantages and events. Surveys of the homeless population identify two distinct groupings: firstly, a homeless population who use homeless services such as hostels, and secondly, those categorised as homeless by the local authority and living in temporary accommodation.

The former group (the traditional homeless) is predominantly male (75%) and the majority (53%) of the latter group are women with children (Williams and O'Connor 1999). Male service users are primarily single (or separated), they tend to be homeless for longer and to have transient accommodation patterns (Cleary and Prizeman 1999). There is little possibility of accommodation stability as few apply for local authority housing (Fahey and Watson 1995). The age profile of the male homeless population is changing and young people are increasingly in evidence (Cleary and Prizeman 1999). Homeless men also tend to be poorly integrated socially; in general, they have few support networks and relatively little contact with families. Disengagement from family and community increases, as one would expect, in line with duration of homelessness. They frequently have a long history of unemployment preceded by minimum schooling and often ill-health and substance abuse problems (Holohan 1997; O'Brien and Moran 1998; Feeney et al. 2000). In one study almost half (48%) of the homeless people interviewed had a mental health difficulty and approximately two-thirds had made a serious suicide attempt (Cleary and Prizeman 1999).

Homelessness occurs usually before the age of thirty years. Nearly three-quarters of a sample of homeless people in Dublin had become homeless by this age and a fifth had become homeless by the age of 16 years (Cleary and Prizeman 1999). The pattern tends to be one of a progression from childhood to homelessness rather than a drop into homelessness in later life. The main reasons for initial homelessness include parent-child conflict, escape from problematic home backgrounds, relationship breakdown and substance abuse. Leaving residential care (Kelleher, Kelleher and Corbett 2000) or prison (Cleary and Prizeman 1999) and or a failed transition to employment and independence are other major factors (O'Brien and Moran 1998).

Men who are homeless have generally been out of work for some years and the pattern is usually one of casual employment giving way to a complete cessation of work. Their economic and educational difficulties are generally compounded by personal and health problems. Some of these difficulties originate in their childhood and some, especially alcohol and substance abuse, often begin before or soon after leaving school. Transitions from school to work to establishing independence are often difficult. At an early stage substance abuse becomes entwined with crime in order to maintain the substance habit (Dillon 2001).

Involvement in crime

Although Ireland is, by international standards, a low crime country, there has been a considerable increase in the level of crime over the last three decades (McCullagh 1996). Crime, in Ireland as in other countries, is predominantly a male phenomenon and 95% of the prison population is male (O'Mahony 1997). Offenders tend to come overwhelmingly from lower socio-economic backgrounds but more particularly backgrounds where extreme social and economic disadvantage is evident. In one study, 28% per cent of prisoners experienced parental separation as children and 12% lost a parent through death before the age of sixteen (O'Mahony 1993). Very low levels of educational attainment and vocational experience are also common. Up to 80% of a prison population in one study had left school before the age of sixteen and over a quarter had never had a 'proper' job (O'Mahony op. cit). Literacy levels amongst this population are a good deal lower than the general population (McGivney 1999). Involvement in crime starts early. In O'Mahony's study (op. cit) over three-quarters had been detained in the juvenile system. Substance abuse and psychiatric problems are also common.

Debates around troubled masculinities invariably, as Hearn (1998) says, involve a discussion of crime. These debates centre on the recognition that it is men, especially young men, who predominate in crime statistics. However, crime is not committed equally by all men but (at least identified crime) varies socio-economically and spatially. Crime is concentrated among men from lower socio-economic backgrounds and those with a low level of education, vocational and employment skills (O'Mahony 1997). Crime is also heavily concentrated in certain geographical, usually urban, areas. McCullagh (1996) rejects the notion that the increase in crime has resulted from the undermining of traditional systems of social control. A more likely explanation, he suggests, is that social change has increased both the opportunities for criminal activity and also the size of the pool of potential offenders. The reason working class men are more likely to become involved in crime may be related to the economic marginalisation of some working class men resulting from labour market changes. In this perspective crime is a form of adaptation to marginalisation as well as an attempt to overcome it.

Substance abuse

As with offenders and the homeless, the majority of known substance abusers in this country are male and relatively young. The average age for first treatment contacts was 20-23 years in a study by Geoghegan, O'Shea and Cox (1999). Drug users (at first contact) tend to be unemployed and to have poor educational levels (early school leaving is common) and work experience (Geoghegan et. al. op. cit). There is a strong link between socio-economic status, especially economic disadvantage and drug use (O'Brien and Moran 1998; Dillon 2001). Drug users also tend to come from similar areas. This influences initiation into drug taking. This usually takes place at a young age (usually about 13 years) and is shaped by exposure to drug use, availability and peer networks (Mayock 2000).

There is a convincing association between substance abuse and crime and it is estimated that drug-users account for a significant proportion (perhaps a majority) of detected crime (Keogh 1997). Dillon's (2001) analysis demonstrated how users initially view drug use as recreational and pleasurable but as dependency grows they are drawn into taking opiates to avoid withdrawal symptoms. This invariably forces them to become involved in crime as the demands of their dependency increases. A study of drug users arrested for criminal activity revealed similar findings as well as a comparable profile to other marginalized groupings such as the homeless (Keogh 1997). Drug users were overwhelmingly male with low levels of educational attainment and work skills. Almost half (47%) were fathers. Almost three-quarters (73%) had started using drugs before the age of 18 and the majority (58%) had been in contact with the law before the age of 16 years. Cannabis was the initial drug for the majority but just over 30% started with heroin. The two main income sources for the group were social welfare payments and criminal activity underlined by the type of crimes committed (burglary, shoplifting etc). Approximately half of the participants had family members also involved in crime. There was also evidence of health problems in that almost a quarter of the sample had been inpatients in a psychiatric hospital, 28% had made a suicide attempt and 10% had tested positive for HIV.

The link between crime and drug use is evident from this and other sources. Drug activity begins early, usually during adolescence and is generally associated with involvement in crime. Both groupings are drawn from similar populations. They tend to lack educational and job skills, are often early school leavers and are overwhelmingly from disadvantaged backgrounds and districts. These features are also evident in homeless populations. Poor levels of education, followed by little or no vocational training, followed by lack of success in the job market and a background of personal, familial and health difficulties appear to be common features. This would seem to point to similar pathways to homelessness, crime and drug abuse as well as the association of these marginalized lifestyles.

Summarising points

❖ Homeless men are generally single and lack integrative and support networks. Homelessness begins early in life and is caused by a variety of factors mainly family and relationship related. Poor health and substance abuse also feature.

Homeless men tend to come from lower socio-economic groupings, exhibit very low levels of educational and job skills and have a poor employment record.

❖ Men similarly predominate in crime statistics and the increase in crime over the past three decades in Ireland may be related to the economic exclusion of working class male groupings. There is a strong link between detected crime and socio-economic disadvantage. Young, working-class men, especially those from disadvantaged backgrounds, are over-represented among offenders. This may however be a feature of the way crime is defined, detected and recorded. Crime is also associated with specific geographical, disadvantaged locations.

❖ Drug use is closely linked to crime and both drug users and offenders tend to come from similar, disadvantaged backgrounds – though the misuse of drugs is by no means confined to those from such backgrounds.

❖ Comparable features identified in homeless and drug using populations as well as among offenders point to similar pathways to homelessness, crime and drug abuse.

1.5 Changing Value Systems and Psychological Marginalisation

In the preceding sections the impact on men of various aspects of social change has been examined. This section considers changing values and belief systems in Ireland and the psychological consequences of this plus other social transformations.

Religious beliefs and secularisation
In Ireland values have been heavily influenced by a particular belief system due to the predominance of the Catholic Church and religion has been viewed as a strong integrative feature.

Consequently evidence of changing beliefs and values has been linked to theories of value disintegration and psychological alienation.

A dramatic shift has occurred in religious beliefs and practice in Ireland over the last three decades and this is particularly evident in the 1990s (Inglis 1998). In 1974 the national figure for mass attendance was 91% (Nic Ghiolla Phádraig 1992) but in 1999 this had declined to 59% (Cassidy 2002). Church attendance is a good deal lower amongst younger cohorts (Cassidy op. cit). In 1981 three-quarters of young people (18-26 years) attended Mass weekly in contrast to less than a quarter (23%) today. Yet the present level of church attendance is high by international standards and religious belief remains an important feature of Irish society (Fahey 2002). It is clear however that adherence to the institution as well as the moral authority of the Catholic Church has weakened considerably, especially amongst the young (Cassidy op. cit).

The decline in religious observance has been viewed as symptomatic of a move towards a more individualist, secular society and recent analysis has provided some support for this view (Cassidy op. cit). An increasing attachment to individual freedom and responsibility is evident in this country yet there remains a strong commitment to social, communal goals (Cassidy op. cit). There is a trend towards individualistic values, as well as a privatisation of belief, but no evidence of extreme individualism (Cassidy op. cit).

Belief and value change is apparent across all age groupings in the last two decades but there are considerable age differentials in relation to some matters (Breen 2002). Amongst young people in particular there is an explicit rejection of Church authority in relation to moral values along with an acceptance of liberal, secular values (Breen op. cit). This move towards more secular and liberal values is associated with an acceptance of suicide, which is often identified as an indicator of alienation in a society. The youngest age cohort (18-25 years) is much more likely than older cohorts to consider suicide justified. But there is a gender difference evident here in that females are significantly more likely to regard suicide as 'never justified' than are males (61% in contrast to 43%). There is some suggestion that the reduction in communal values and religious allegiance, apparent in the younger age cohorts, is connected to lower levels of well-being and to contemplation of suicide (Breen op. cit). According to Breen there is a slight indication that the rise in liberal and secular values alongside the increased acceptance of suicide might be indicative of decreased happiness and increased alienation especially among young men.

Values, integration and psychological marginalisation

Shifts in moral concepts and values, as well as the rapid political and economic reforms which have affected societal cohesion, are cited as causes of increased psychological disorder. Individualism, it is proposed, leads to increased risks, especially for young people in transitional periods of their lives (Rutter and Smith 1995; Eckersley 2001). Suicide might be regarded as an expression of individual freedom and control over one's life (Eckersley and Dear 2002). At a societal level, individualism is strongly correlated with subjective well-being, and societies where these features predominate have higher suicide rates (Veenhoven 1999; Eckersley and Dear 2002). Suicide, especially youth suicide, rises as social conditions and personal prospects improve which indicates that increasing personal freedom can have both desirable and undesirable consequences. The majority of citizens may benefit from these developments but a minority, especially those with fewer resources at their disposal, may not profit. The costs of being excluded are likely to be higher in societies where most people are empowered and this is especially so for men, who are more likely than females to relate their status to others in a society. Thus when those around them are perceived to be better off than they are, young men are more likely to consider suicide

(Barber 2001). The costs of individualism may be offset for young women by improving social status and economic participation as well as by their greater social connectedness (Cross and Madson 1997).

Individualism may also be associated with a more general sense of alienation amongst the young in society. There are suggestions that well-being among young people has declined (a fact evidenced by increasing rates for attempted suicide) (Eckersley and Dear 2002). Similarly Beck (1992) and others have spoken of the uncertain, fragmented, nature of life and relationships today and the differential accumulation of risk factors across class lines. Prevailing norms of personal autonomy and attainment may be unattainable for some. But while aspects of individualism appear to be associated cross nationally with youth suicide there are other, usually more culturally specific factors involved. This is indicated by the variation in the rise and fall of rates between and within countries. Declining rates of suicide in some 'individualistic' countries probably imply adaptation to change.

The pattern of rapid social change experienced in Ireland since the 1970s and the concurrent rise in the suicide rate (from a previously very low level) have led to a proliferation of attempts to link the two phenomena (Kelleher and Daly 1990; Kelleher, Chambers and Corcoran 1999). These efforts have either focused on general social change or specific aspects of societal transformation such as the decline in religious observance. The possibility of a link between religious beliefs and suicide remains attractive since its elaboration by Durkheim (1951 (translated)) two centuries ago. There is evidence that religious adherence is protective in relation to suicide (Breault 1986). It is unlikely however that religious adherence is the only explanation and attempts to test this hypothesis in Ireland have not proved successful (Kelleher et al. 1999). Other aspects of social change such as the increased labour market participation of women have been examined primarily because of the preponderance of men in suicide statistics. This latter phenomenon may have resulted in less emotional and practical support for men (Stack 1998).

The main focus of attention in this area has been on young men because of their greater propensity to complete suicide. The rise in Irish suicide rates differs markedly by gender and while male rates have increased considerably since 1970 the female rate has remained stable and low. This reflects patterns in other countries. Males are more vulnerable to suicide at every age but are most at risk between the ages of 15 and 24 years. The increase in male suicide has been linked to various aspects of social change. The link between male suicide rates and the movement of married women into the labour force has been cited above as well as the implications of changed work environments for men. There is in some countries an association between suicide and a rise in substance abuse but in Ireland the regions with the highest suicide rates have the lowest levels of substance abuse (Kelleher et al. 1996). Other explanations have centred on differences in male and female roles. It is suggested that women possess more protective features in relation to suicide.

Females are more connected than men to others both socially and psychologically. Women see themselves as interdependent, men as independent and separate (Cross and Madson 1997). For men marriage and the family can often be their most important source of belonging and this is probably why they are so affected by relationship break-up (Departments of Public Health 2001). Because males are less likely to be integrated in confiding friendship networks they do not have the channels to express distress (Duncombe and Marsden 1993). Sexual and relationship freedom brings additional challenges. As Inglis has said in relation to sexual norms in Ireland, it may be that the demands of contemporary sexuality, of being sexually active and attractive, "are just as demanding, if not more so, than being chaste and pure" (Inglis 2002, p.166). There are well mapped, socially acceptable, ways for men to behave and in some instances suicide

50

may be viewed as appropriate masculine behaviour (Canetto 1997). One of the male participants in Owens (2000) study remarked "For most men, when something happens, they would take the suicide route rather than admit they are weak." Males may also be more likely to complete suicide because of the lethality of the methods although this is disputed (Canetto 1997). Differential gender attitudes to religion have been cited as protective in terms of suicide (Stack 2000a). Women appear to internalise religious values more than men while males seem to be more attached to the structural, institutional features of religion. This may be important in relation to Irish suicide rates in that females seem to have retained a greater degree of spiritual and religious belief than men as the institutional church is declining (Cassidy 2002).

Another possible risk factor for men is their greater involvement in marginalized groupings. People who are socially and economically excluded are more likely to engage in suicidal behaviour. Economic disadvantage appears to be a more important risk factor for men than for women (Barber 2001). Suicide rates are significantly higher amongst marginalized categories such as the unemployed and the homeless (Cleary and Prizeman 1999) or those experiencing economic marginalisation and loneliness as in rural Ireland (Connolly and Lester 2000; Ní Laoire 2001). Among those who attempt or complete suicide both economic and educational deficits are apparent (Kelleher 1998b). Single and widowed men are more vulnerable to suicide as are men who have separated from spouses and partners (Departments of Public Health 2001).

Summarising points

- There has been a significant decline in religious participation among Irish Catholics and, most obviously, a rejection of religious authoritarianism. These trends have been identified as a move towards a modified form of secularisation and are most obvious amongst the younger age cohorts.

❖ Attitudes to moral issues have changed substantially across all age groupings in the last two decades but there are considerable age differentials in relation to some matters. Young people demonstrate more liberal values overall. There is increased acceptance of suicide among young people and this acceptance is more obvious amongst males.

❖ The pattern of rapid social change experienced in Ireland since the 1970s and the concurrent rise in the suicide rate (from a previously very low level) have led to attempts to link the two phenomena but there is no clear association between general or specific aspects of social change and the rise in the suicide rate. It is unlikely that there is a single causal explanation for suicide but national and international trends are apparent.

❖ Explanations for the increase in male, but not female, suicide have centred on explanations around traditional male roles and behaviour, in particular their lack of access to confiding networks and their inability to disclose distress. Economic factors may be implicated in terms of changing patterns of male employment and married women working which has affected male roles both within and outside the family. Those who engage in suicidal behaviour are more likely to lack economic resources and to have low levels of educational skills. Men appear to be more affected by their relatively poor position in the economy. Finally males may be more at risk of suicide because of their membership of marginalized groupings such as the homeless and those who abuse drugs.

1.6 Conclusions

The first part of this report has examined some of the key evidence about how men and boys fare in the areas of the family, education and work. Marginal lifestyles and psychological alienation were also addressed. This has helped to highlight some of the important factors which influence the process of marginalisation for boys and young men in contemporary Irish society. In summary, the review of the current context has revealed that:

❖ *The Family:* Changes in the family have affected all families, all children and all men in Ireland. There are now more families headed by lone mothers, even though these represent a minority of family units. The contention that children in families without a father are psychologically and socially damaged is empirically difficult to sustain. Much of the discourse about absent fathers fails to recognise the diversity of fathers and fatherhood now in evidence. The term 'absent father' usually implies absence of 'a good father'. Despite the undoubted importance of fathers children can survive the loss of either parent. It may be however that fathers outside the home have gained least from the family changes described, in that marriage may have become less available to them. There are some empirical links between lone parenthood and troubled male children but the key variables in all families appear to be the ability of the parent to parent, the quality of parenting and socio-economic status. When these features combine negatively, where there is a serious lack of parenting combined with other features especially poverty, then children in both lone and two-parent families may be vulnerable. Lone parent families may be more at risk because of a dependence on one parent and because lone parent families are more likely than two-parent families to be economically disadvantaged. Boys may be more affected, or appear to be more affected by problematic family situations because of differing and gendered manifestations of distress, e.g. behavioural and conduct problems. These are more likely to come to the attention of parents and teachers because this behaviour is difficult to tolerate. Boys with these difficulties at home or school are more likely to become involved in out-of-home and school subgroups that tend to be linked to anti-social behaviour and alcohol or substance abuse. Whether the young man becomes embedded in this lifestyle is dependent on a number of factors including his personal, educational and economic resources.

❖ *Education:* Young men from working class backgrounds are more likely than females and other Irish males to drop out of the educational system early. Gender and social class interact closely here. Males in general are performing less well educationally than females in Ireland but not all males are equally affected. Boys and young men from lower socio-economic groups are much more disadvantaged than boys generally. Males from these backgrounds do less well because of early difficulties experienced in home and school environments and or because of specific learning difficulties. There may also be an antagonism between educational attainment and the achievement of traditional and valued masculinities. These factors combined make it more likely that boys from working class backgrounds will disengage and drop out of the school system altogether.

❖ *Work:* The decline of traditional male work areas alongside an increase in job sectors accessible to both men and women have transformed the labour market in Ireland and elsewhere. This has had implications for men both in the home and at work. Men face greater competition in the labour market and a considerable number still enter traditional work areas despite the economic vulnerability of these sectors. This and other routes which some men follow may result in economic marginalisation. Young males who leave school with no qualifications are more at risk of unemployment than labour market entrants with a Leaving Certificate. Men from lower socio-economic backgrounds are greatly over represented amongst this grouping and these young men are doing significantly less well in the job market than men from higher socio-economic backgrounds. These elements make individuals susceptible to long-term unemployment and feature also in the profiles of other economically marginalised groups such as the homeless. Economic exclusion has far reaching consequences in that it affects the ability to set up an independent home and family.

❖ *Marginalised Lifestyles:* Certain similar features can be identified in different marginalised groups, in particular the homeless, those who abuse drugs and offenders. They are predominantly male categories. Poor levels of education, followed by little or no vocational training, followed by lack of success in the job market and a background of personal, familial and health difficulties appear to be common elements. The similarity of characteristics apparent in the various marginalized categories point to similar pathways to homelessness.

❖ *Changing Values and Alienation:* Changing values and other social transformations have prompted debate around themes of alienation especially amongst young people. This has arisen in response to the co-occurrence of considerable social change and a rise in the suicide rate in this country. There has been a decline in religious participation and influence. These trends have been identified as a move towards secularisation with more liberal value systems and greater individualism evident. This is especially noticeable amongst younger age cohorts but there is no evidence that these changes have resulted in widespread alienation amongst young people. There is however greater acceptance of suicide (which is usually correlated with higher rates of suicide) and this is more obvious amongst young males. Young men are more likely to complete suicide, and explanations for this have ranged from the impact of work and family change on men to masculine behaviour and expectations - in particular men's lack of confiding relationships and their inability to disclose problems. Men who attempt or complete suicides are more likely to be single and to have low levels of educational and work skills. Males are also more at risk because of their membership of marginalized groupings such as the homeless, partly because the rate of suicide is much higher in these populations and also because males appear to be more affected (than females) by their relatively poor position in the economy.

The Experience of Marginalisation: A View from the Margins

A Qualitative Case Study of Young Men Out-Of-Home in Dublin

2.1 Introduction

This section of the study focuses on a group of young men who are out-of-home. They are described here as marginalised because of their homeless status. The aim of this chapter is twofold. Firstly, the objective is to examine some of the issues raised in chapter one to see if they emerge in the lives of the men. Thus factors such as socio-economic status and family background, educational experiences, precipitants of homelessness and involvement in drugs and crime will be examined. Issues around masculinity and behaviour associated with traditional masculinities will also be explored. Secondly, the aim is to allow these men to recount their experiences of living on the margins of society. The rationale for this section of the report is the necessity of listening to the voices of those who are marginalised in order to understand and conceptualise this phenomenon.

2.2 Methodology

The study employed a qualitative research framework. In-depth interviews were conducted, over a two month period in 2000, with

58

a consecutive sample of twenty homeless men between the ages of 18 and 30 years who were attending a drop-in centre for homeless men in Dublin. Access to participants was facilitated through the drop-in centre. Staff requested all men attending the centre (in the selected age group) to participate in the study. There were two refusals. The interviewer then explained to the participant the nature and purpose of the research and asked if the interview could be tape-recorded. All of the men agreed to this request.

The interviews were based on a semi-structured schedule. This schedule was developed following a review of relevant literature and in line with the aims of the research study. Two pilot interviews were carried out using a draft schedule. It followed the themes of childhood and family background, school, work, homelessness, social networks and relationships, substance abuse and criminal behaviour. On completion of the interviews all tapes were transcribed and analysed in terms of both the schedule themes and issues that emerged from the interview process.

Prior to the commencement of the study the research proposal and final interview schedule were submitted to the drop in centre for ethical consideration. The research plan and schedule were approved by the centre, subject to minor changes.

This chapter follows the themes of the schedule. First, experiences of childhood, family and school are explored. Then, the interviewees' experiences of leaving home, moving towards homelessness, coping with living out-of-home, links with crime and drugs, experiences of, and attitudes to, living out-of-home are detailed. The findings are essentially presented in the men's own narrative - the story of their lives up to now. A selection of short profiles of some of the interviewees is included and are interspersed throughout the text to illustrate some of the issues raised. All names have been changed to protect the identities of the interviewees.

2.3 The Path from Home to Homelessness

Childhood and family background

A clear association between contextual themes that were presented in chapter one of this publication, and these men's lives emerged from these interviews. The men were overwhelmingly from the lowest socio-economic groupings. Only one man came from a middle class background. Reflecting their socio-economic background, the majority (17) of the men came from districts identified as disadvantaged. Only two men came from areas with a mixed socio-economic composition. Nineteen of the men came from the greater Dublin area (from both the city centre and the suburbs). One was from Northern Ireland and had come to live in Dublin in the last year.

The family backgrounds of the men indicated extreme disadvantage across the social, economical and psychological spectrum. Only four of the twenty men came from families where both natural parents were still living together in the family home, with no reported addiction or domestic violence. Their early lives were characterised by events of trauma and loss. This small group had a long list of negative events and difficulties, which perhaps most crucially, tended to cluster in the lives of many of the men. Their stories illustrate the impact of such factors and how they tend to overlap and create a certain trajectory.

The men interviewed had experienced, usually at a young age, a range of significant negative events and difficulties including death, family separation, reconstituted families, domestic violence, parental mental illness and addiction, and care placements. Seven participants had lost a parent (usually a father) through death, and one man had lost both parents. The way in which the parent died was also indicative of disadvantage. One father's death was alcohol-related, another was drugs-related and a third father died of hypothermia while sleeping rough. Eleven of the twenty participants experienced family separation, usually when the father left the family home.

Four men were raised by mothers only, with some of the difficulties encountered by lone parents evident here (although they had very positive experiences, in general, of their mothers' parenting skills). The quotes below demonstrate how a child without other support systems may be vulnerable in such situations. Two men did experience alternative support; for example a grandmother stepped in when a parent was unable to look after the child, and this appeared to have ameliorated the situation.

> I rarely seen much of her, there was no security there...I became a very insecure person...My mother was out working all the hours God sent. We were going to the neighbours, my sister and myself, looking to get fed and washed. (Alan)

> [She] worked her bleedin' fingers to the bone...worked two or three cleaning jobs all her life, to give us everything, our house was the nicest house on the street...We never had like social workers around the house or anything like that, the house was always spotless...She never smoked or drinked 'cos she always wanted to put away money and get us better stuff or to have better things. (Donal)

> Me mum's ma...she was sort of like a mother to me as well, 'cos when me ma would run off...you know with her friends, me nanny would take me in, me nanny would feed me. (Mark)

> Two of me brothers and me sister lived in me nannie's, me and me other brother lived with me ma and me da..It wasn't that me ma neglected them, my house was only up the road from my nannie's...it was just like two houses, like I often lived in me nannie's for a few weeks or a few months and then went back to me ma's. (David)

Four men had experienced reconstituted families in that they had lived at some point with a step-parent, usually a stepfather. They had to adjust to the step-parent's role and authority, cope with conflict between their biological and step-parent and negotiate issues of identity and rejection. Reconstituted families gave rise to complex family structures, several men having half-siblings. This also raised questions of family identity and belonging.

I'd be thinking: he's not even me dad and he's telling me what to do...Probably sounds stupid, but things go through your mind, and I get very upset at things like that...It was hard for me to class him [step-father] as me dad, but when I thought about it he was there...from when I was two years of age. The other fella I haven't seen in what - 18 years. (Mark)

My ma and my da, they had me...and my mother had other kids before she met my da, so there's a good few of them, and me da has met a woman since then, like years ago and he's had kids with her, so I'm in the middle. I've half brothers and sisters on both sides and when I count them all up there's about 21 of us, but we all count each other as brothers and sisters. (Donal)

Neil

Neil is in his mid twenties. He was placed in care when he was ten after having run away from a difficult home situation. He got on well in care and completed his Leaving Certificate. He became homeless four years ago when he left a flat to find accommodation with a girlfriend. Unable to find a place to live, the relationship broke down. He has continued to work while homeless. He has a child from a subsequent relationship and he became homeless again when they separated. Neil has never had a problem with drugs and has never been in prison.

Three men had been raised in-care and this proved to be traumatic in a number of ways. Firstly they described the experience of entering the care situation as traumatic. This involved a conflict of loyalties between their attachment to their families and their need to escape abusive family situations. One man had to face these conflicts in a particularly traumatic way when, aged ten years, he was asked in a social worker's office to choose between his family and a care placement.

> Me da was sitting right there and I had to turn around and say: "Yeah, I don't want to go home, I'm going into child care", I had to say that right in front of them and...that was it. (Neil)

The second traumatic element of care centered on the breakdown of care placements which all three had experienced a number of times. These placement breakdowns had a profound effect on these men and gave rise to feelings of displacement, insecurity and a sense of 'failure'. Another potential consequence of being in-care was the weakening of familial ties and potential support. These factors were compounded when, as happened with one man, the child went directly from a foster care situation to institutional care. In this man's case we see an example of a trajectory outlined in chapter one of this publication, where different negative events and situations cluster. Another theme that emerged from the men's narrative is a sense of inevitability, of being unable to 'get off' a preordained pathway.

> It [the placement] just never worked out. [I] was too violent in those days, so they sent me home, I'd leave home then... (Robert)

> I don't know where I stand, 'cos [I went] from just one home to another home to the streets, to hostels, to jail...never being in the one spot too long. (Patrick)

There's sixteen in my family. So, I know about six of them, I've never met the rest of them, they're all over the place. I don't really know still to this day, to class meself as a Traveller or not...so, I'll just be who I am. (Patrick)

Patrick

Patrick is in his mid twenties. He grew up in residential and foster care. From the age of 12, Patrick began drinking and was expelled from school. At 14 he spent four months on his own sleeping rough. He was placed in residential care but at 16 he became homeless again. Patrick has been homeless for about eight years and has spent a number of years in prison. There was domestic violence and alcoholism in his family. There was also violence in his foster family.

From a very early age there was evidence of violence in the men's lives. Half of the participants reported that there was violence and abuse within their families when they were growing up, with five of these families also affected by alcohol addiction. In all but one case the perpetrator was a male. Sometimes the violence was directed at the mother only, but in other families it was directed at both mother and children. In two cases the abuse was aimed at the child/interviewee only.

When I was born my father was beating up my mother so as soon as she came out of hospital she was forced to move away from him... [she] thought that if she didn't leave that we would all be going into care. (Brian)

He [father] was of a violent nature, always sporadic violence...towards me and my sister and me mother. (Kevin)

There was a lot of violence, everyday. Nearly everyday he used to come home drunk and batter her. (Patrick)

Me ma was violent with me...me ma used to open the door every morning and I'd stand in the front garden [of a neighbour's house where he was staying] and she'd shout: "Oh you scumbag!" and all. (Barry)

Another dysfunctional feature was the lack of a permanent home. During the interviewees' childhood, several families moved houses, sometimes frequently. This tended to increase the sense of dislocation or rootlessness already caused by a difficult home environment. In some cases the families experienced an episode of homelessness. One participant lived with his mother in a refuge until the age of five. Homelessness was often linked to one or both parent's drug or alcohol abuse or to violence (e.g. a mother leaving a violent relationship and bringing the children with her). One man, whose parents are both addicted to heroin, described how the community rejected the family because of his parents' behaviour. This community rejection, which may be a feature of the lives of such children, no doubt increased the child's sense of alienation. Following the eviction, this man and his younger siblings were separated from their parents and placed in foster care with relatives. He is now addicted to heroin.

Me mam got evicted, she got evicted for anti-social behaviour, which is the kids basically running amok and the neighbours making complaints about the kids, and then three complaints and that's it, you are out, three strikes and you go. (Mark)

Barry

Barry is in his late twenties. There was a history of alcoholism and domestic violence in his family. He ran away from home at 13. While homeless (spending some time living with a neighbour) he continued to go to school and sat his Group

Certificate. He began using drugs as a teenager after the death of a friend. He has spent a number of years in prison. He is currently sleeping rough and is a heroin user. However he hopes to get off heroin and improve his relationship with his girlfriend and child (who are not homeless).

Parental addiction problems were a common feature. These usually involved alcohol addiction (six men) but also included drug addiction, as described above. There was also evidence of intergenerational addiction.

Me mother is a chronic alcoholic. Every day of the week, from nine in the morning...till eleven at night, she's in the pub. Me father died from drink three years ago. He was living on the streets, I've never met him...I've three or four brothers that are bad alcoholics as well. (Patrick)

My grandfather is an alcoholic and my da was an alcoholic and my stepfather. (Kevin)

All me da's side is all like drug addicts, bank robbers and thieves, they are all in and out of prison and that's me aunties as well as me uncles. Then me ma's side of the family, they are all drinkers, they're all alcoholics. (Donal)

The prevalence of addiction experiences in the lives of so many of the men has affected them in different ways. Apart from deficient parenting and the economic and psychological effects of such a home, it may also have exposed them to a culture of addiction, an environment where such usage was possible, even acceptable. Although alcohol was the usual form of addiction in the home, the child may have been influenced towards drug use. A majority of the participants were drug-users. In addition, a more direct effect of addiction in the home was the fact that two of the men were introduced to drugs by a sibling. This supports the drug-related research findings presented in Chapter One.

> Me sister was strung out on Es, she bought me my first E for me 16th birthday. (James)

There was also evidence of intergenerational homelessness.

> (My da) was on the streets in London and for a while as well...[He was] only on the streets for about six months but he still knows what it's like...and he'd be telling me stories of when he was in London. (Robert)

To what extent did the factors described above contribute to the present circumstances of the men? As the above illustrates, a substantial number of the participants experienced significant disadvantage and trauma in their early lives. During a time when children are laying the foundations of future skills and self-esteem, the participants were living in environments, which, as identified in chapter one, are not conducive to the development of these primary resources.

Those who experienced family instability and loss during their childhood were very conscious of its effect on their lives. Throughout the interviews the men frequently expressed a sense of deprivation due to childhood difficulties. Yet the majority of children, including male children who have had such experiences do not become homeless or socially deviant. Children are active social agents and often prove resilient and creative when confronted with such difficulties. Similarly there is no particular arrangement of factors, which are mandatory in the lives of children and young people. However certain features such as psychological and social security do help provide the foundations for self-esteem and other skills. The absence of these, as well as economic deprivation, in the lives of many of the men, perhaps created a vulnerability to, but not a certainty of future marginalisation. Neither can one easily identify lone parenthood as a determining feature. The men raised in these families had generally very positive experiences of their mother's parenting skills. The multi-problematic nature of their young lives, with difficulties, which were, in general, quite outside their control emerges from their narratives. In making links between their youth and later lives several lines of causation are possible.

For example, as a consequence of their disjointed early family experiences many of the men have fragmented family relationships and a weak system of family support. This lack of social support may, in the absence of any alternative, have proved a continual negative feature in their lives. In order to understand the complexity of this issue we need to examine how the men responded to family and other difficulties. One way of coping with a problematic childhood was to repress one's memories and emotions, to disconnect one emotionally.

What my mother did to my father, what my father did to my mother, I never talked about that to anyone and I never will. I've dealt with it myself over the years slowly but surely in my own mind. (Neil)

Some of the men responded to violence or other difficulties in the home with anger and sometimes with violence.

There were killings between him [father] and me ma all the time. He was giving me ma a fuckin' box, pushing the head off her basically. So I attacked him a few times with a hammer...I just don't let anyone hit women basically...It got to the stage where I said: "Right, I'll give him a few slaps or whatever and have a fight with him so he won't hit me ma", but then after that I'm going to go out and do something and whatever it was, whether I robbed a car or broke into a shop, I'd take all the stuff out of the shop and bring it all back here and annoy him...as revenge. (Eamon)

I though that was the right thing to do, you know what I mean, as a kid like, you come in and get drunk and smash the place up, and my thinking was that's what you do when you're drunk. (Joe)

Another compensatory route was to take on the paternal role oneself.

They [brothers and sisters] looked up to me more than they did me dad, 'cos I think me dad was an easy-going person, they knew they could get around him, but they knew they couldn't get around me. If they started messing or anything, me ma would just call me and say: "Will you sort them out, they're wrecking me head". (Mark)

Some of the participants reacted to problems at home by flight, leaving home in early adolescence. One man ran away from home at 11 years of age. Many looked to alternative sources of affirmation outside the home, and peers began to replace family as role models and as a source of identity.

At this point some became involved in drugs and crime. This often had serious implications for school life and participation, as we will see when we review school experiences. What is apparent from the stories of these men is that many of them were experiencing distress and displaying behavioural problems from early childhood. Some recognised that they needed help.

I started on drugs at an early age, at a very early age; I started smoking hash first when I was nine. Then I was just smoking hash and drinking, and as that was going on I was robbing cars and building everything up, you know what I mean. Then I started on harder drugs when I was 13...on naps [morphine], stayed on them till I was 17, was off them once for 6 months, and then straight into heroin. (Eamon)

Since I was four or five years of age, I never felt like I was getting what I should be getting, and that was help. (Patrick)

Evidence that family difficulties were impacting on the children is provided by the problems that were also manifest in the lives of siblings. Some were taken into care, a number of older siblings served time in prison and addiction problems were also evident amongst siblings.

Relationships with fathers
The effect of childhood on the men is strongly demonstrated by their relationship with their fathers. The above narrative has shown that many of the men were raised in households where there was violence, with the father generally the perpetrator. Some also experienced fathers who were alcoholics or addicted to drugs. Others were raised in households where there was no father figure or perhaps an intermittent male parent figure. Eight of the twenty men either never met their natural father, or did not know their fathers in any meaningful way when they were growing up. One man described his father as "in and out of the house" because of his drinking. These departures often left behind feelings of abandonment and unresolved rejection and bitterness, with some of the men rejecting efforts by their estranged fathers to re-establish contact.

I know him to see, but I don't have any contact. If I met him in a pub I would kind of step aside, but I'd say if I talked to him and told him who I was and the situation I'm in, he'd probably take me in. But I just wouldn't be able to stay in the same room as him, it'd make me sick, you know, 'cos I know what he did to my mother and all...she had a really hard life. (Brian)

He used to pop his head up every now and again like. He tries now more than ever to see us but I have no

time for him. He's a scumbag as far as I'm concerned.
He left my auld one and just me and me brother, two
kids, a one-year-old and a six-year-old. (Donal)

You don't just walk into someone's life after 18 years
and turn around and say: "I'm your da, welcome,
come on and I'll take you under my wing". I don't
want him to come near me. (Joe)

Many of the men expressed a feeling of loss because they did not have a close relationship with their father. Some mourned the physical loss of a father but many spoke about the loss of a father figure they could look up to. Many reported that they had never had a role model "to look up to".

That's my problem, I've never had a role model, 'cos
I never had a father...As long as I can remember it's
been I've always been looking for this role model
person, be it a boyfriend of my mother's or an older
person. (Alan)

I never had anyone behind me to say: "Look, this is
the right road to life, this is what you do". You know
what I mean, a grown-up, someone with a bit of
experience to turn around and say, you know: "Get a
job, settle down, do this". I never had anybody like
that. (Mark)

Some of the men responded to this lack of an ideal parental model with anger, for example, if the father suffered from a psychiatric illness. In one case a participant assaulted his mentally ill father, causing him to leave home. The father then became homeless and subsequently died of hypothermia. The participant's words illustrate his feelings of sadness and loss about his father and perhaps refer also to his own homeless situation.

I felt that he shouldn't have been there, he should have been in his own home, he shouldn't have died at all...he shouldn't have been cold, he should have been in a warm bed. (David)

Many of the men, as indicated above, either had no relationship or a poor relationship with their fathers. Some had difficulty communicating with them at any level. A number mentioned that their fathers were unsupportive or rejecting towards them.

Seán

Seán is in his early twenties and grew up outside Dublin. He got on well in school but left home due to conflict with his parents. He became homeless when he could no longer afford a flat. He has never had a problem with alcohol or drugs nor has he ever been involved in crime. His family are unaware that he is homeless, as he says he feels too ashamed to tell them.

The way we're talking now, having a conversation, I've never done that with me father, never, ever, never sat down and had a conversation with him. I just don't see eye to eye at all. (Joe)

I always looked up to him, always respected him, but he never showed any emotions, never, I never seen my father drunk, I never seen my father cry. He was always "Shut up, do what you're told", you know that kind of way...He's never expressed himself in front of me or the rest of the family: he's just a typical man. I couldn't go talk to him about problems, it wasn't his thing, he wouldn't have been able to cope with it, you know. (Seán)

To compensate for the lack of male role model, some men sought alternative male role models or took on the father role themselves.

Others spoke of "looking up to" older brothers and friends, as well as musicians, footballers, and TV personalities.

> *He's dead now but the Manager of Liverpool...I used to use him as a father figure, instead of my own father. (Joe)*

Relationships with mothers

Relationships with mothers were, in general, more positive. The majority said that they were close to their mothers and considered them to be supportive. But mother-son relationships were sometimes conflicting, especially if the mother had been abusive, or had treated them unfairly.

> *I love me ma as well (as my father), (but) I just can't handle her, she's done bad on me. When she dies I'm not even going to be there at her funeral. The damn witch, I hate her even though I still love her. (Barry)*

School

There was a clear trend among the participants to leave school early. A number of factors were involved here. Some men, for example, had difficult school experiences. However the most common theme in relation to school was its lack of significance, the minimal impact the educational experience had on these individuals. The most notable feature of this section of the interviews was the lack of narrative. Many of the participants had little to say about their school days. They gave the impression that school had been a 'non-event'.

> *I didn't really go to school, to be honest with you. (Mark)*

Almost all the men conformed to the well-mapped educational trajectory for marginalised people. The continuing effect of early school leaving on their employment prospects, as described in chapter one, is very evident at this point of their lives. Thirteen of the twenty participants had left school before the minimum leaving age (16 years) without any qualifications or vocational skills.

Two participants had completed the Leaving Certificate or equivalent (GCSE) and five others left school after Junior, Intermediate or Group Certificate examination. Some of the participants left school at 14 years to work - in one case because the family needed the additional income. Many participants reported that they were "kicked out" of school usually at 13 or 14 years (one had been excluded from school at the age of 11 years), or left voluntarily because they "just couldn't cope with it". This usually happened in first or second year in secondary school. The decision to leave school and its timing were often closely linked to the onset of drug abuse.

James

James is in his late teens. He was suspended from primary school for causing trouble and left school at 16 just before his Junior Certificate. He has had a series of jobs since then. James began smoking hash at 13 and continues to smoke daily. He also takes Ecstasy and has dabbled in other drugs. He left home because of conflict over his drug use. James slept rough initially and later moved into a hostel, but continued to work.

(I left) around the time I started heroin...I couldn't handle going to school anymore. (Donal)

Difficulties in school started at an early age for many. Some men had very negative memories of school.

I could never take, eh, orders...I could never have somebody saying to me do this or do that. Even though they're trying to help, I wouldn't understand...I could never agree with being put down, you know what I mean. 'Cos I always thought I was being put down so (I got) detention nearly every day. (Patrick)

I'm not ashamed to say it, many a time he had me sitting crying my eyes out in that office with the pain. He used to (make you) hold out your hands and whip your hands with a ruler. (Donal)

However, despite negative school experiences, some participants expressed regret at not finishing their education. Some made a connection between leaving school early and their present circumstances.

I wouldn't be in this predicament now...on the run from the police and into drugs. (Michael)

In many cases the participants had poor attendance records, and when they did attend they were reprimanded for their behaviour. This increased their marginalisation in the classroom and led to further disengagement from the system. During their time in school they failed to connect either with the teachers, their fellow pupils or the educational system in general. Eventually, "in the interests of the rest of the class", they were excluded from school.

I had such a bad temper so I kept getting bleedin' violent with the other kids and teachers and all so eventually I got kicked out. (Robert)

They used to say that if I wasn't leading the messing that the others wouldn't be messing. So it was always, like, me being picked out of everybody else. (Donal)

The majority of the men were not in any way angry at the school system, or felt that their particular school had failed them. In fact the participants in many cases felt that they themselves had contributed to their school difficulties and often used the term 'messer' to describe their behaviour in school. The decision to leave school also appeared to involve an active choice albeit usually following a period of drifting towards the margins of school life.

It is clear they did not buy into the educational system and that they did not particularly enjoy school. School was not seen as necessary to their future and they did not make the connection between success in school and future occupational success. However, judged from their point of view it may have been a rational and even positive choice - taking an alternative pathway when the existing route proved impossible and/or irrelevant. Issues around educational frameworks and the relevance of the school curriculum to working-class students may be important here but are probably not the only issue. The ability to learn is also key. Some of these men indicated they had had such problems and other studies have shown a high level of learning difficulties among the homeless population (Cleary and Prizeman 1999). There are also gender factors involved (McGivney 1999; Corridan 2002). Young working-class women are increasingly availing of educational opportunities but young men from this background less so. The explanation for this lies partly in the continuing adherence of young working-class men to traditional masculine behaviours which are becoming increasingly outmoded (Mac an Ghaill 1994).

> ...Like, the other kids that I hung around with when I was younger were sort of in the same boat as meself, like. Their das were missing, and most of them had big families and their families were struggling as well, you know what I mean. So they were sort of ... like school wasn't, like [for them], they had no time for school, they had no discipline at all, like. (Donal)

Some of the young men made a connection between their poor performance and misbehaviour in school and their difficulties at home. At least one man linked his educational difficulties to a specific learning disability.

I went through a phase...I just wasn't getting on with my father. I was never going to school. If I did go to school I'd only be in the school half an hour and I'd be sent home or get suspended or expelled...I was always in trouble in school. (Eamon)

I don't know whether (it was) Attention Deficit Disorder or something like that, but he [the teacher] just couldn't hold my attention in school. I used to get bored really quickly. I still do to this day, can't keep me attention...five seconds and me mind is wandering off. (Donal)

In sum, the young men left school for a number of reasons; because they had no interest in school, because they recognised they were not sufficiently skilled to cope with the educational system, because problems at home made it difficult to cope with schoolwork, because there was no back-up or encouragement to continue their education, because they wanted to go on to other things. A combination of these factors was usually apparent in their lives. For some an involvement in drugs and or criminal activity was also important. All of these points have been raised in chapter one of this publication.

Leaving home

The early emergence of problems was evident in the lives of the men. By the time they reached adolescence a number had been in contact with various services for behaviour difficulties. Some reported attending school counsellors, others talked about being "always in trouble", or of being excluded from school due to their behaviour. By the age of 15 the majority of the men had deviated fairly significantly from the usual pathways and transitions through adolescence into adulthood.

While other young people of their age were accumulating educational and vocational resources, some of the men began to accumulate negative points in terms of moving on to work and gaining independence. From their stories they appear also to have lacked from an early age a strong sense of self-identity - a fact no doubt related to their difficult, sometimes abusive, home backgrounds. Their descriptions of the route into homelessness highlight the fact that causation is usually multi-dimensional. Some men left home in order to escape from a difficult situation, with the aim of creating a more positive social and emotional environment for themselves.

Personal and family difficulties then became intertwined with structural problems around gaining employment and finding affordable living accommodation. Failure to gain employment made finding a home more problematic, and, if there was a transitory accommodation phase, friends, peers and the sub-culture increased in importance, with alcohol and substance abuse often emerging.

Frequently however, involvement in drugs while still in the family home occurred and this often precipitated leaving home. Sometimes the men left home simply to lead independent lives. At this gateway to homelessness, some themes can be identified. A problematic home background is an important common feature among these homeless men. This probably affected their chances of gaining a strong sense of self, which in turn affected their ability in school. In addition, many of the men lacked a positive, male role-model. However not all families were problematic and such families offer a profile of how parents try to cope with difficulties in their children, as well as highlighting another marker on the road to marginalisation - drug addiction.

Five families appeared to have functioned well until the adolescent stage of the men. There was no apparent conflict and no obvious loss events such as separation or death. But the parents in these families did not appear to have the skills to cope when a son's behaviour became problematic and he started getting his own ideas in life. By no means did all of these parents ask their son to leave home, and at least one actively tried to prevent the young man departing. However, relationships often deteriorated to a point where the man was forced to leave home. This was especially so when drugs and or criminal behaviour were involved. Families generally had great difficulty understanding and coping with a son's addiction problem.

Peter

Peter is in his early twenties. He attended school and college and worked until his drug use, particularly the use of Ecstasy, became a problem. He began smoking hash at 13. He began using Ecstasy while working and, as his usage became heavier, his relationship with his family deteriorated and he eventually had to leave home. He has been living in hostels for three months. Peter is currently clean, following a residential detox. However he says that he intends to resume his Ecstasy habit when he can afford it. Peter has not been involved in crime.

I was the first child to say: "I'm moving out and doing my own thing from now on", and I think it kind of scared my mother 'cos she didn't want me going at all. It took me two days to get outside the house, so it did, to actually get out the front door. She had the front door locked, she had my room locked, she had me da trying to nail the door so I couldn't get out, she was taking it really bad. (Seán)

He [father] didn't understand me, he didn't understand me at all, he didn't. He didn't know how to take me, I was his little babbie...he looked after me more than the rest of the kids. You know what I mean, and I ended up like that [taking heroin and involved in crime]. (Michael)

Getting kicked out of home

The men made a distinction between leaving home voluntarily and being kicked out. Many participants were kicked out or thrown out of home for what was considered to be their anti-social behaviour. This was usually linked to drug-use or criminal activity. Many families tolerated their son's behaviour at first, but at some point relations deteriorated and the son was asked to leave the house. Sometimes the reason was the threat he posed to the family, especially the younger children, or because he was endangering the parent's mental health. There was a sense here that the families excluded and sacrificed one child in order to 'save' other family members. Sometimes a particular event gave a parent a chance to evict the son or stop him from re-entering - e.g. release from prison. These families were either unwilling or unable to allow the young man to remain in the house and in some cases the family's reasons were understood and accepted.

Colm

Colm is in his mid twenties. He left school at 14 and began a trade apprenticeship. At this stage he began to experiment with drugs. He left home due to conflict with his family and has been barred from the family home. Colm has no convictions but has been in court a few times.

They asked me to go 'cos I was in stolen cars, doing burglaries, doing robberies. It was the drugs and the police kicking in the hall door, it just got too much for me ma.. Me ma had had a quadruple by-pass two years ago... she's a bit better now, 'cos I'm out of the house, I still go up to see her, I love her. (Michael)

I was just coming home drunk all the time, and all that. There was too many arguments, so I just left. (Patrick)

I took a few things that I shouldn't have out of the house [jewellery] *and sold them* [for drugs] *and I came*

> *back that day and they [his parents] said: "Look, we can't have you here anymore"…. I haven't been back since, they kicked me out that day. (Joe)*

Substance abuse was the direct cause of homelessness in some of these men's histories. Drug abuse acted as a precipitant to homelessness and thereafter contributed to them remaining homeless. There was a high rate of heroin addiction among this sample of young men but progression to heroin sometimes followed their entry into homelessness. Participants involved in drugs tended to maintain ties with their families and continued to visit their former homes. They are still welcomed into the family home and so often do not consider themselves "really homeless".

> *I wouldn't really describe myself as homeless 'cos I always have a place to go, … it's through my own fault that I'm like this. If I got off drugs I'd always have a place to stay…I'm always in and out of the house, now any time I come out of prison I do go home for two or three weeks and then I do leave again [due to heroin use]. (John)*

> *Its been happening for four years on and off, kicking me out and taking me back and giving me chances…[I go] back home, they give you a chance, oh you're doing brilliant. Back then on the gear, we're going to have to ask you to leave, your mother's worried. Me ma had two heart attacks and she's on a heart monitor at the moment. (Joe)*

When a break with home was as a result of their own behaviour, the men often perceived these relationship breakdowns as personal failures and had subsequent feelings of regret. Many expressed guilt at the negative effect their behaviour had had on their families. In some cases they recognised that their behaviour had destabilised the family.

I got them into it [heroin] really...I started, brother started, sister started, brother-in-law started, aunties and uncles started, just a big dirty ball, no control. (Michael)

She [mother] ended up having to move out of (name of place) because of me and me brother being on drugs and all. (Donal)

A couple of months after [he left home] she had a heart attack and I quietened down...for about a year and a half, but I was still on the drugs, but I wasn't going out and doing what I was doing for the drugs. I actually got a bit of work, so I was just going to work but I was strung out.... She was happy with that, she calmed down and everything was grand, and then I just went chaotic again. (Eamon)

I've had run-ins with gangs...gangs jumping out of cars, weapons, bars and everything, there was murder a few times...it wouldn't affect me, but it would affect me mother. (Colm)

Escaping abusive home situations

Several of the men first became homeless to escape an abusive home situation. At some point their parents' behaviour became unacceptable, forcing them to leave the family home. Two participants ran away from home when they were young adolescents and were taken into state care. Another participant became homeless at 14 when his care placement broke down. The transition to independence usually failed because of the often precipitous nature of the departure and the lack of planning involved (combined with a lack of money and job skills). Leaving home often followed an argument, with the result that there was little time to arrange alternative accommodation.

I couldn't handle the two of them...fighting and all that; I couldn't hack it so I'd just disappear. (Barry)

When I was 12 that's when I first started (leaving home), I got kicked out of my da's... (Robert)

Some of the men, who were kicked out due to their unacceptable behaviour, described their conduct as a response to parental abusive behaviour.

I didn't like what he [father] was doing and it annoyed me. And for me to take the anger out I was going out to do something else, say I went out and robbed a car...and I'd come back and if me da had been pulling with me ma and if he hit her, I'd hit me da. I fucking fought me da from the age of 13... (Eamon)

In the short-term quite a number of the participants established some form of independent living away from the family home. However, in the longer term they were unable to maintain their independence. This failure was often linked to their addictions, either alcohol or drug abuse. But it was also linked to financial difficulties, relationship breakdowns and the ebbing away of support. Absence of family assistance combined with lack of affordable, rented accommodation made homelessness a real possibility. Sometimes they had failed to rent in the private sector, which compounded their difficulties locating work and then found it increasingly difficult to re-establish themselves. Their lack of money made them susceptible to other negative events. Thus one man was forced to live in a hostel when his landlord sold the rented property and held onto his deposit. Another precipitant of homelessness was release from prison.

It was difficult 'cos when I came out of prison, like, I'd nowhere to go basically... I was on the streets... This would be the first place I came to [the centre] .... Its where all me friends and all are now…This is the first place I came to, didn't even go near me family, fuck the family basically. (Eamon)

When you are in prison a lot you aren't actually going forward with the world. When you come out, it's just reality smashes straight into your face. (Eamon)

The reasons for leaving home, elaborated here, are diverse but a number of clear trends emerged. Firstly, a number of the men were forced by their families to leave home, most frequently because of drug use (sometimes combined with criminal activity). In these cases drug use was the main cause of homelessness but families often retained contact with their son. Escaping an abusive family environment, or a home where there was inadequate parenting due to illness or substance abuse, was another precipitant. Alternatively, those with problematic family backgrounds, drifted into homelessness from subsequent care situations. Both these groupings appeared to be the more disadvantaged in personal, educational and other terms than the other men. Another identifiable group consisted of those who left home to seek independence but failed to make the transition successfully. Finally, some entered homelessness following imprisonment.

2.4 Homelessness

The length of time the men had been homeless varied from a first episode of three months to 15 years. As members of the group were all in their twenties, for some this implied continuous homelessness from early adolescence. Recurring episodes of homelessness over a number of years were a feature of many life histories. Some of the men had returned to the family home at intervals but this rarely lasted very long.

The participants spoke of their experience of being homeless, of the loneliness and isolation, of the lack of support, of the physical discomfort of sleeping rough, especially in winter, and of the health problems they suffer as a result. All the men remembered their first experience of being without a home.

> When I was out of the flat on the first night, I had nowhere to go and I had no idea where I was to go. I had never heard of homeless hostels or night shelters. I had led a very sheltered life...I spent the first two nights on the streets, eating scraps, just trying to get by... [Another homeless man he met told him about a hostel]. (Seán)

Most participants had experienced different forms of accommodation, such as sleeping rough, staying in hostels or B&Bs, and living with friends and relatives. They differed in their opinions of hostels, the main form of accommodation, in that some liked the social contact there but others found hostels too restrictive.

> I tried all (of) them. They wouldn't work. I don't like them. You have to queue up at four o'clock in the day. I prefer to have my freedom and that's being honest. (Robert)

Coping with homelessness

The extent to which these men become excluded from society is dependent on a number of factors, some alluded to above. Economic and housing factors are crucial but so also is the ability to maintain contact with family and to develop and sustain relationships with sexual partners. Friendships are important as are contacts with professional agencies. These links help to avoid hopelessness and are thus protective of mental health. There was wide variation among the men in relation to the levels of support received.

Partners, girlfriends and fatherhood

Relationships with partners were central to the participants' stories and for many the core relationship was with a girlfriend. Relationships with children and families were also viewed as important. Partners often offered the men support and assistance in improving their lives, giving up drugs, seeking help etc.

> If I didn't have a girlfriend I'd have been dead, I'd have killed myself... She's the only thing keeping me alive really. (Peter)

Many men mentioned the positive influence of their girlfriends or other women on their behaviour. One participant attributed his success in breaking his shoplifting habit to the influence of his girlfriend. They also spoke of women having a calming influence on their violent reactions.

> I was very violent when I was younger, from 17 up to 20, very violent, anything, anything could trigger me off... ...Women, women settled me down. I got a girlfriend and she didn't like me fighting. [She] talked to me a lot. I never used to go to the cinema or anything and she'd say: "Come on, let's go to the cinema or for a walk". (Joe)

The difficulty of sustaining relationships with partners and families was a common theme among the men. The problematic nature of relationships when one is without a home is exemplified in their experiences and attitudes to fatherhood. Nine of the 20 participants were fathers but their involvement with their children was generally minimal. None were currently living with their children and only two of the fathers were still in a relationship with the mother of their child. Some of the children were being reared by the mother alone or by a relative, in all cases a relative of the mother. One child had been placed in care, as both parents were homeless. Although some expressed sadness at this situation, in general fathers appeared to accept it as an inevitable consequence of their homelessness.

> On the streets it's hard 'cos I don't really get to see him as much unless she brings him into me. I ring her up and say: "Will you meet me in town with the babe?" ... (We'll) probably go up to the park for an hour or two and sit down and talk. (Robert)

> I find, to be honest with you, the hardest thing is that I don't get to hear the child cry at night. You know the way parents do get used to that, you know what I mean. (Robert)

> I'd love to be able to communicate better with my son... I want me son to be able to come to me to ask me what he wants or if there's something wrong with him, but he still doesn't. He's only four years of age, but he's not coming to me... he'll ask me girlfriend [not the child's mother]. (Eamon)

Having children was a strong feature in the lives of these men even if they were not actively involved in their day-to-day lives. Some fathers do want more involvement with their children and a few have tried to increase contact. A number experienced problems in relation to parental access, with one man having to obtain permission through the courts to see his child. Many of the fathers viewed their child as a positive influence in their lives and something to live for. They want to protect their children from knowing about their past and current situation, but feel that in the future the child will "wanna know who her father is".

> She gives me energy, you know when she gives you a little hug or stuff like that... I don't want her to know much about my past, you know. (Kevin)

I love me son to bits, I'd do anything for him, I just don't want him going down the same road I went down, I don't want him going through all this, don't want police coming to the door. (He can) smoke a bit of hash if he wants, I don't care but (not) anything else. He can drink, but I'll never throw him on the streets, I'll make sure he's never on the streets. (Eamon)

I had a row with (my girlfriend)… and she told me I wasn't allowed to see me kid anymore. So I just flipped and tried to kill myself. First time I ever done anything like that… (but) I didn't want anybody to turn around and say, well your father killed himself, he od'd. I just don't want me kid to ever hear anything like that. I want her always to think that her father is a good man. I don't want to buy her love either, I just want her to love me for what I am, you know. She is only young yet so she won't really understand, but before she's six I want to make something of meself. I wanna be the father she always dreamt of. (Barry)

In many cases the men's aspirations for their children reflected difficulties in their own family backgrounds.

If I had a son or daughter I'd give it a totally different life than what I had, (at the) emotional level, talking, communicating, sit down with them, bring them everywhere. My father never done any of that. "Are you coming out to have a game of ball da?" "No, no". (Joe)

I'll never slap him, I'll never raise my hand to him… I'll never give him a reason to run out of the gaff… I'll never let that happen… I'll never put a kid in a position like that where he'll be on the streets. (Robert)

My kids will never be on the street, if they end up on drugs I'll help them instead of beating them. (Barry)

Being a father facilitated connectedness with the world outside homelessness. It was also perceived as a stabilising factor. This was equally true for those who did not have children. All those who didn't have children, said they would like to be fathers one day – some commenting that now was not the right time to have a child because of their homelessness or their substance abuse.

I'd like to have kids. It'd be harder but the responsibility and all would get me away from all these drugs, I know that for a fact. I've seen it happen to one or two, but then they'd relapse again. If I had kids I'd stay off the drugs for good 'cos I love kids. (John)

The situation of the men and the views expressed by them in relation to fatherhood underline changes which have taken place in the family in Ireland and elsewhere. Women are increasingly raising children alone and the gender and power implications of this was acknowledged by them.

(In) today's world... I won't say man is the provider. Going back a good few years ago I would say yeah, but, today no, I'd say the woman is more the provider at the moment, as with money coming into the house and physical things... How would I class a man? Basically a lazy fucker... To be honest with you, I fear women... things they can do like give birth, that frightens me. I'm not the only one, it frightens a lot of men. They are just better than men basically. (Eamon)

Women are getting more aggressive, it's a positive thing for the girls but bad for the blokes, they could take over… probably do a better job. We nearly killed the place. Youse can have the world, wash it, iron it and give it back to us. (John)

Men used to speak ill of them… years ago. Now women just won't have none of it. Now they just lash back and the men are stuck for words. (Brendan)

Family and friends

When relationships with family and others are not maintained a process of isolation may develop in which the man becomes increasingly disconnected from his former social world. Either the family or the man himself may instigate this process. The man may be 'blanked' by his family and friends or the man may cut himself off from his former social connections due to embarrassment. This isolation from both family and former friends pushes these men further away from normal life, closing off avenues of social contact and holding them within the homeless world. Complete loss of contact with family generally has a profound effect. Many of the men had weakened family systems as a result of deaths, separation and conflict or through having a care background. Relationships were often weak in the first place and if conflict with family preceded homelessness, this exacerbated the situation. Several of the men felt that their behaviour had alienated their families and continued to do so.

She [his mother] won't answer the door, all the curtains are closed in the house… everything is boarded. It's like boarded up, literally. (Another day) I went over to try and talk to her and she just ignored me and I kind of lost the head, not real physically but verbally, lost the head with her, trying to tell her what she was doing, asking her what her problem is, why she won't talk to me… On another occasion, I lost the head and threw a brick through the window. It was out of frustration, when you are sleeping rough and you are going around people's houses you say to yourself: "I'm better off in prison". I just sat there waiting for the police to come up. (When they arrived they told me) there was a barring order issued against me. (Colm)

(My brother is) very different to me, like he was brought up really well, I don't think it would be fair for me to, you know, go into his life, the way I am now. When I come off the drugs I would like to see him. (Brian)

Me relatives all just blanked, the minute they hear the word heroin, (they) just leave me in the corner. ... All me neighbours despise me, every one of them, and that worries me ma. (Joe)

Some men (especially drug-users) found that former friends ignored them which they perceived as an expression of disapproval.

(He was) probably my best friend... He's blanking me now, he's all: "I'm too busy I can't meet you". He's saying: "Right you're a scum, you're below me, I'm better than you now"... I don't need friends (Peter)

[Former drug using friends] don't want anything to do with anyone on heroin, they were the same as I was and now they are totally different, they wouldn't entertain me. If the word 'heroin' popped up, they'd just walk away. (I find that) very hard, 'cos they were like me at one stage and now they are just ignoring the fact that they were there. (Joe)

Participants were sometimes embarrassed by their circumstances and homeless status. As a result they purposely avoided contacting old friends, fearing their reactions. This sense of shame can also prevent them from seeking help from family members and hence narrows their social world. Embarrassment also interfered with their ability to seek professional help. A number of the men said they were too proud to ask for help or did not want to burden other people with their troubles: "you get sick of hassling people". One participant spoke of keeping his use of social and medical services "to a minimum", as he is "embarrassed".

> I try to do that [get in touch with old friends] as little as possible... and I won't be telling them that I'm homeless. (I tell them) I've a lovely gaff, great job, doing great for myself... its people I've grown up with all my life I don't want them to think that I've fallen into some sort of a trap. That I'm lower than they are. ...I feel ashamed of myself... I don't mind telling other homeless people that I'm homeless. That's the only kind of people I would really tell. (Seán)

> I wouldn't put anything like that on anyone's doorstep. (Robert)

> I wouldn't even walk through [name of home area] like this, I was always spotlessly clean. (If) I'm walking through town I'd be afraid to see any of me friends. I sold all my clothes, sold them for tablets. (David)

Some participants had remained in contact with friends who have been a source of support. Friends who maintain contact are often those experiencing similar problems. There were also practical obstacles, notably hostel hours, to maintaining social relationships with those outside this population.

> They take you in at six o'clock and that's you for the night, there's no social life with it. The only social life

a homeless person can build up is with other homeless people. (Seán)

Isolation from their family, friends and former social worlds affect the men's self-confidence and identity and creates a sense of dislocation and rootlessness. Some participants however had become completely isolated, reporting that they had no one with whom they could talk.

I never had anybody to turn to if I was ever feeling down or if I had any problems. Or well, I could turn to me ma but it was just, I don't know, I just felt like if I'd turn to me ma, I'd feel embarrassed, I'd hold it inside, it made me a little more wise. (Mark)

When I feel low, I feel low, you know what I mean, I try hard not to beat myself up, I just go and sit somewhere and just think and think and think, and I say to myself: "No I shouldn't be thinking of this, and I go for a walk and try to forget about it then, you know". (Patrick)

The above quotes underline an important aspect of relationships and friendships, the ability to confide in someone. Having a confidant, a person to whom one can disclose one's experiences and fears, is protective of one's well being and identity.

It's good for you to get things out of your system, 'cos if you bottle all that up you could damage somebody or you could damage yourself. (Barry)

A number of participants reported having a confidant, often a family member, girlfriend or friend. Others had support from specific workers, such as addiction counsellors, or workers in voluntary homeless agencies. These workers are often very important supports in these men's lives. One man explained that he wouldn't (or couldn't) cry in front of his girlfriend as he feared upsetting her but he feels free to cry, and has done so, in front of his female support workers. The participants also alluded to the difficulty men have in disclosing problems. Several participants commented that they found it easier to express themselves emotionally to a woman rather than to another man, both in personal and professional situations.

Brendan

Brendan is in his late twenties. He left school at 14 to take up work. Brendan has been a heroin user since he was 15 and recently started a methadone programme. He has been to prison and became homeless following a relationship breakdown. He has young children whom he sees regularly. He is hopeful that he can get off drugs, find housing and become reconciled with his partner and children.

> I don't know if I identify more with women... I wouldn't say some things to men that I would say to a woman... I don't know what it is, if it's just because I've never had a proper role model (for) being a man. (Patrick)

> It's just, it'd feel weird, a bloke expressing his feelings to another bloke, nay, it wouldn't be me. (Eamon)

The lack of support from family and former friends prompted some to make friends amongst other homeless people. They describe a mixture of strong friendship and distrust among the homeless population. There is a tendency to befriend those in similar circumstances to oneself. Thus the men generally befriend others in the same age group who are using similar drugs. For some there is a sense of belonging and some level of trust in this world. However the issue of trust/distrust was raised by many of the participants.

> There's no trust, there's never any trust, I wouldn't turn me back for a second. (Joe)

> I don't trust nobody. I hate saying that. I should trust somebody but I don't, I can't. I won't let meself do it. (Patrick)

Another possible source of support, institutional religion, was not an important feature in the lives of most of the men although several commented that they had a belief in God or a spiritual life. Religion was mentioned as important by one participant as it helped to keep him positive and another made the connection between religion and the religious who work in the homeless services.

> I think it's important in this life to believe in something, you know what I mean, there has to be something to believe in, otherwise everything we do is for nothing. Being homeless I'd go [to church] everyday, even if there's no mass on, I'll go in and say my own quiet prayers... A few times suicide did cross my mind but it wasn't tried, 'cos what it comes down to is because of my beliefs. If I do this I'd go to hell forever, that strong fear. I think that's the one thing that stopped me. (Seán)

Maintaining an identity
There is, as these men make clear, a powerful stigma attached to being homeless and this affects contact with family and friends, which in turn affects their ability to leave or to get out of homelessness. The individual's attitude to his marginalised status is important, as is the extent to which he internalises his marginalisation. There are many stereotypes attached to homeless people such as involvement in crime and drugs and this can further isolate individuals from society in general as well as from families and friends. Some of the participants spoke of the reactions of the

general public. A number of the men begged or 'tapped' for money but found people's attitudes difficult to cope with.

> *If you are walking down the road and you're walking past some woman, she'll grab hold of her handbag... I'm used to all that, I don't mind it at all... [People] got a right to be negative, haven't they, 'cos they'd rob the eyeballs out of your head, you know what I mean. (John)*

> *They'd look down at you, as if you were dirt at the bottom of their shoe, and (say): "Get a job", and: "How can one live like this?" (Joe)*

> *I was begging once... [on] Ha-penny Bridge, the hot spot, it was Sunday (and) I was looking for money to pay the (hostel) rent money, so me and a couple of friends went tapping to get the money up to pay that night. It was the most degrading thing I've ever had to do in my life. Big time, yeah, 'cos there's a lot of snide people about, you know, funny remarks: "Get a job". That was my most degrading moment, let me down the most. It's the last thing I ever thought I'd see myself do in my lifetime. (Seán)*

However begging is a good source of income and can be a source of social contact and some had experienced kindness as well as rejection.

> *There is a lot of nice people out there, (they) wake you up and give you a cup of coffee. (Robert)*

> *You get to always talk to people... lovely people who sit down and talk to me and go up and buy me a McDonald's and all. Even if someone threw a penny into me jar, it's the thought that counts you know. (Barry)*

96

The extent to which homelessness impinges on one's self identity depends on several factors. These factors include self-definition, perception of one's homeless state, one's reactions to social exclusion and the ability to maintain or re-create one's former identities. The men in this study employed different coping mechanisms to deal with stigmatisation and maintain an identity. One response is to "ignore 'em".

> I couldn't give a damn... I just walk around town as if I own it. It's my bedroom and if anyone has a problem with it just boom, boom, boom. (Colm)

Another participant blanked out negative attitudes with the philosophy that there's a thin line between him and those who are "all high and mighty. I have a house, you mightn't always have it. One thing and you can lose the whole lot". Many of the participants attempted to distance themselves from the label of homelessness by differentiating their homeless status, by maintaining that it was a temporary situation.

> This is temporary, just a temporary arrangement, a setback. (Seán)

> I am homeless, but I wouldn't like to think of myself as really really down in the dumps, homeless... down and out... I just like to think of meself as having a spot of bother... and I'll work myself out of [it]. (Mark)

Viewing one's situation as temporary usually involved a distancing from older, homeless, men who were perceived as in a hopeless state. Another distinction was made between those who had given up drugs and those who were still abusing.

> I know that I am homeless, but I haven't ever considered myself that I am... I've no intentions of staying there [in a hostel]... The people out there [in

the centre] don't think like that you know. I'm just more sensible, I suppose, in that way. (Brian)

They are out on the streets for the rest of their lives, most of them old fellas don't give a shit... no self-confidence... I know I'm not going to live on the streets for the rest of my life. (Mark)

A few participants emphasised that their identities were not defined by their homeless status. Their core identity was still intact.

It's still mother-son... it's not like 'cos we are on the streets things change. We still do the exact same things that we would if we were living at home, probably go shopping, whatever, go have something to eat. It's not like 'cos we are living on the streets everything has changed. We still live the same life we do live if we were living at home. (Mark)

I think of myself as a man first, but if I have to sleep out I'll sleep out and don't really call it homelessness because I can find people's houses to go to, but I don't want to be a burden on anyone. (Brendan)

Another coping mechanism is to use aggression, especially when threatened, as a method of conflict resolution. In the face of obstacles a violent or aggressive reaction is used to express frustration and anger and to retain some level of self-respect. Sometimes anger is directed at hostel authorities (one participant spoke of having "battered" the hostel manager when he was kicked out for smoking cannabis) but the most frequent site of potential confrontation is with Gardaí and security personnel. The men felt that being homeless attracted Garda attention as they were so visible around the city. They believed that Gardaí and security people targeted them.

> *They have this stereotype they have. If you are a Dublin man and you're under twenty-five, you must be on heroin. (Neil)*

> *I walked into a shop with a girl… I was never in the shop before (but) the security guard grabbed me by the scruff… and just flung me out the door… for nothing… for just walking into the shop. Things like that annoy me. Things like that make me do life in prison for. (David)*

These practices are interpreted by the men as a form of discrimination and harassment. Several participants spoke of the public humiliation of being searched by the Gardaí and questioned the validity of the searches.

> *You are lucky to do through a night without getting searched… No reason, nothing at all, just to torment you, that's what I think anyway. They've an attitude problem, just 'cos they've got the suit on. (Eoin)*

> *They're more or less looking for if you're carrying drugs. That's what they say, they're doing a drugs search or whatever, you know, I've had the same two policemen stop me three or four times and search me for drugs, when they know I don't take them. (Patrick)*

These incidents led at times to confrontation with Gardaí and some claimed they had been assaulted by the police. Others react to what is perceived as a violation of rights by becoming verbally or physically abusive. Those who referred to themselves as "more experienced" said they had learnt to temper their responses.

> *I used to snap years ago, I used to always end up in custody, but now I just talk to them, get it [the search] over and done with real quick. You either get charged or you're let go. (Barry)*

A final category of response to marginalisation is to opt out, either by increasing use of alcohol and drugs or by suicide. Two participants mentioned contemplating suicide when their circumstances were particularly bad. Some of these tactics further marginalised the person by leading them deeper into substance abuse, violence, criminal activity and convictions. Some distanced themselves from their own behaviour by inferring that they had little or no control over it: "It was the E, it wasn't me".

> Me mate who hung himself he's probably better off where he is, you know, but it's sad to see. (Kevin)

> Who knows, maybe I'm better to take this road in life, not to be losing the head all the time 'cos (it) causes a lot of trouble. I've fallen out with friends, and had fights... At the moment I'm probably in a way happier than I ever was 'cos I have my freedom... It has its advantages and disadvantages. (Colm)

> E destroyed my fucking life, destroyed my career, destroyed my home... I haven't given it up in the slightest. The only reason I got this new job is so I can afford to buy it again I don't really care, if I'm going to die I want to die happy. I'll be lucky to live to my 22nd birthday if I keep going. I don't care, I just don't care. (Peter)

Surviving homelessness for the majority of younger participants involved retaining a hope that they would escape from this situation.

> I know all I want from life, and that's why I'm going to make it happen, just try and get a job, get me own flat, I've been trying these things, but the thing is they just don't seem to fall into place. Hopefully one day it'll fall into place... I just have to take it day by day. I

*am not going to plan the future, 'cos every time I plan
the future it doesn't seem to work for me. (Mark)*

Substance abuse

A link between homelessness and substance abuse is evident from
the men's stories. Only three of the twenty participants were not
involved in substance abuse. Thirteen participants were, or had
been, addicted to heroin, seven are currently intravenous (IV) heroin
users, six are on methadone maintenance programmes, and one of
these was also addicted to alcohol. Two men had alcohol problems.
One participant was addicted to Ecstasy in the past, but is now
clear and one young man is a heavy cannabis user. Several
participants were poly-users and cross-addicted, using a mixture of
tablets such as 'benzos' (benzodiazepines), sleeping tablets,
Valium, alcohol and heroin (a practice which is potentially lethal).

Eamon

**Eamon is in his late twenties. He says he began smoking hash
when he was nine, later he began drinking, robbing cars and
using other drugs. He has a difficult relationship with his father
who was an alcoholic and abusive towards his mother. He has
been using heroin for nine years and is currently on a
methadone programme. Eamon left school when he was 15
and has spent several years in prison and several sleeping
rough. He has a young child who is in the care of his ex-partner
and with whom he has access visits. He and his current
girlfriend are in B&B accommodation.**

Sixteen participants spoke of undergoing some form of
detoxification for their drug use. For those with addiction
problems, drug use dominated their lives. A number had
experiences of overdosing and had been hospitalised but this did
not deter them from using drugs. A high prevalence of substance
abuse was found in this sample of men, but other studies of the
homeless population in Dublin suggest that the prevalence of
drug use is lower than that indicated here (Ó Moráin, 1999).

The men had started using drugs at a young age, sometimes a very young age, and had used a variety of drugs, often moving from smoking cannabis to injecting heroin by 16 or 17 years of age. Hence many have been addicted to some substance for a substantial period (with one person being addicted for 14 years). Many of the participants commented that they had chosen to take drugs. They mentioned that their drug use was linked to the dance scene. Some spoke of it as being an escape from their circumstances, "a way of getting out of it all". One man said that drugs helped his self-confidence.

John

John is in his mid twenties. He left school at 14. By his late teens he was using heroin. His father was an alcoholic. John is sleeping rough and has been homeless on and off over the past five years. He has been in and out of prison for shoplifting to support his heroin habit. He has a good relationship with his mother and siblings.

It was there so I just started taking it...I just liked taking them...felt good.... it wasn't that it was peer pressure or anything. If I didn't want drugs I wouldn't have taken them. (John)

It's hard to explain, I just done it, you know to escape from (name of area) or something. (Kevin)

I was very shy around people, I'm not now but I was then, when I was young when I was coming up to 14, 15, 16. I was very shy around girls and all. And now I'm not. I wasn't peer pressured. I wanted to see what it was like and I liked it, it made me feel more confident. (David)

Of the three men who had no addictions, all had dabbled in drugs of some kind and one still smokes cannabis occasionally. Two of the young men described their drug taking as a phase, something they had moved on from.

> I've done them all before, I've tried them, been through it all... for me it was just a phase. I was one of the lucky ones on the day, I was lucky to get away from it. It does affect you psychologically, mentally and physically, it's torture. When I was going through that phase I would have been 18 or 19. I'm 24 now. It's years [before] you come back to reality. (Colm)

Some of the participants recognised the negative effects of drugs.

> We were the best of mates, we were into sports and everything, fit as a fiddle he was, and I see him now, a couple of years later, over by the Corporation there not so long ago, down on his knees in front of his girlfriend.... while she was trying to get the needle in, in front of their two kids. (Neil)

> The alcohol destroys me. Every time I start drinking. I'll be two or three days drinking and it destroys me. (Patrick)

Crime and imprisonment

Almost all of the participants have had some degree of contact with the Gardaí and seventeen of the twenty participants had served time in prison (three on remand). Some participants had spent substantial amounts of their lives in prison, up to eight years in one case. Of the three participants who had never been in prison, one had an outstanding charge and two had been cautioned. There was a clear connection between the former prisoners and heroin addiction, reflecting the findings in chapter one of this report. The three participants without a criminal history did not have a heroin addiction. Although one of these men used Ecstasy, he had not been involved in crime to buy drugs. For the majority of the men their offences were linked to ways of making money, usually involving theft, and were also related to a drug habit ("shoplifting to feed me habit"). Stealing, especially for those with addictions, was viewed as a necessary part of their homeless lives. With a drug habit the survival options are limited:

> When you are on heroin... it's like a demon inside you, you have to feed the beast everyday. (Michael)

> I just rob all the time, like I don't have to do anything else... Before I got locked up I was on £250 a day [€317.50], I had to get up at 7 o'clock in the morning, more than a full-time job, I'd have been better off working actually, you know what I mean. (John)

> If somebody has a habit to feed that's (prostitution) the only road they can go down, or else charge sheets and jail, some people can handle jail and others can't...(Colm)

Many of the crimes committed by the men were directly linked to drugs. They usually involved petty crime ("Mickey Mouse things, stupid things") to pay for drugs. Involvement in serious crime was unusual. Other crimes committed such as joyriding and assaults could be categorised as anti-social behaviour. Criminal behaviour appeared to have an acceptability ranking for the participants, with drug-dealing and mugging rated low.

> (I was) never locked up for drugs. (It was) all cars and jump-overs [robberies over counters]. I done a street robbing, something I should never have done, frightened that woman I did. (Barry)

Some of the men who had been imprisoned viewed prison as a respite from the streets and their problems. For those with addictions it was often seen as a necessary break from their chaotic lifestyles and a time to detox. One man appreciated the "structured lifestyle" of prison "'cos then you can plan your days out, can't you, and have some sort of control". He preferred it to the unstructured chaotic lifestyle of sleeping rough.

> If you are sleeping rough going in there [prison] is like going into a hotel, you have your four meals a day, a gym there. It makes perfect sense. (Colm)

> When you are on drugs you do think about fucking doing things to get caught, when you're homeless... so they can lock you up... to get your head together. (Eoin)

Escaping from homelessness

Many barriers exist which make the route out of homelessness difficult. These include stigma and social isolation, financial problems and the practical difficulties of finding and keeping a home. These difficulties are compounded when there are other problems such as substance abuse, mental health difficulties or criminal behaviour. The initial cause of homelessness is often different from the factors, which prolong it. In one case a difficult family situation was the precipitant. This situation has improved but heroin addiction now makes the man's return home impossible.

> Me gaff is back in order now, it's just me now, I just have to get me self sorted... (Robert)

Getting work

Several participants stated that getting work was the key to "getting back on my feet" but they also saw the obstacles. They were aware of their lack of educational skills. Those abusing heroin described the difficulty of holding down a job when on drugs.

> You can't get a job, when you're ringing up jobs and asking them to ring you back, what do you say? I'm

staying in a hostel! Nobody wants to know when you're homeless... they think it's your own fault for being homeless, (they think you) deserve it, it's crazy, it's totally not true. (Colm)

A lot of employers don't like them [homeless people] 'cos there's so much bad publicity, they are either thieves or beggars or druggies. (Seán)

Finding accommodation

There was little evidence that these men were receiving help towards rehousing. Single men have a low priority on the public housing list and only one participant, who had a girlfriend and children, was on this list. Another participant had a promise of a flat in a voluntary social housing project. A few relied heavily on voluntary services and hostels and showed signs of becoming institutionalised. Most participants turned to their informal support networks and voluntary services in their attempts to re-establish themselves. Some participants expressed their anger at the state system which they viewed as inequitable.

They look after people from different countries better than their own, their own kids. It's very tormenting. (Eoin)

As a consequence of their anti-social behaviour several participants have been barred from hostels. Two were barred from the family home and one from the house where his child lives. This can be a powerful method of isolation. When participants are barred from hostels it reduces their accommodation options, further marginalising them.

I'm not allowed into the house by the police... I'm barred out of the whole area, not allowed in it. I sneak in at 12 and out at half seven... over the back wall job and back over the back wall on the way out... It's hard you know, 'cos you can't just walk in and out of your own bleedin' house. (Michael)

Kicking the drug habit

The majority of participants were engaged in drug use before they became homeless. However, homelessness often led to more chaotic drug-use, which for many was the main obstacle to getting out of homelessness. Participants spoke of drugs being widely available within the homeless scene with resultant difficulties for those trying to give up. The power of addiction and the difficulties of becoming drug-free were noted by several participants, some of who spoke of having switched addictions. They had begun drinking or taking tablets whilst trying to give up heroin.

> *I was only off the plane, I was only in the city, I was standing at the bus stop... I was standing there for two minutes and two blokes came walking up: "Are you coming buzzing are you, haven't seen you in ages". I was only literally bleedin' back ... in the city five minutes and I was being offered the stuff straight away. (Donal)*

> *[The hostel] was worse than being at home, because in the hostel you get up in the morning and there were about four or five heroin dealers at your breakfast table and they're just sticking it in your face, every morning... right in your face. (Joe)*

Overcoming the temptations to use drugs as a coping mechanism, especially when faced with a traumatic event, is one of the challenges in remaining drug free.

> *I got bad news one time and I just flipped and ended up on the gear again... It's easy getting off heroin, it's staying off it that's the hardest thing, that's the struggle. (Barry)*

Participants were critical of the drug services, complaining of year-long waiting lists and the added difficulty of getting a treatment place without a fixed address. They viewed it as a major barrier to their progression out of homelessness. They also had fears about swapping a heroin addiction for the methadone maintenance programme, given the difficulties in withdrawing from methadone.

> I have a reason to do it this time. I just need a little bit of help, and I can't get it. (Barry)

> If you have the determination (you need a place) now. In three months time God knows where you'll be. You could be locked up. You could be dead. (Donal)

Success is possible and a former heroin addict describes the feeling.

> Going back about four weeks ago, me girlfriend had a miscarriage, we were tempted to get heroin ourselves, to try and forget about it, thinking that would take the thought of the miscarriage out of our heads, but we just said: "No, fuck, we won't", and we felt better for it the next day, for saying no…If you can go through something like that and not buy heroin then it's a step forward. (Eamon)

Going straight

Involvement in crime, as discussed above, is another barrier to a person's exit from homelessness. Prison sentences further restrict men from normal social roles and responsibilities. In addition men with a prison record often find it difficult to get employment. The transition from prison back to their normal life is particularly difficult. Changing lifestyles and cycles of behaviour also causes difficulty.

> Getting out of prison, feeling brand new again, then mixing with the wrong crowd and getting back into crime. (Michael)

> *Got out [of prison], back on the streets again, back in there again about two or three months later. (Patrick)*

Cutting ties to a specific group of people and to a specific geographical area is central to breaking a negative lifestyle. Many participants spoke of staying clear of their old neighbourhoods to avoid certain people and to avoid the drug culture in their home area.

> *I haven't been up near (name of area) in over four or five years, and I know if I go back up there even for a half an hour or an hour and I got back into hanging around with the people there that I was hanging around with, I know I'd be back into all the same things. (Eamon)*

Cutting ties to the homeless world

The men spoke of a conflict in relation to their friendships within the marginalised community. Once out of the homeless world, they need to cease contact with homeless people. For some this was a painful thought, as it was perceived as sacrificing one's friends in the interests of one's own survival. For those who have come off drugs it is especially important to break ties with their social circle in order to avoid temptation and remain drug-free.

> *It's a trap. When you get out of being homeless, you've got to keep away from homeless people. 'Cos if you get yourself a flat and you still keep coming here... you're not living a life for yourself, the life you wanted to live, that you got out of the homelessness for. So you have to avoid places like this and people you used to be with, and that's very hard. (Seán)*

Looking to the future

Some of the participants had a very clear image of what they wanted in the future. They spoke of regaining some form of normality, they wanted to restore broken relationships with ex-girlfriends and to see more of their children – to become "a father" again. They recognised the need to change in order to re-establish themselves and reach these goals.

Mark

Mark is in his early twenties. There is a history of heroin use in his family. He left school at 13 and as a teenager he was in and out of juvenile detention. He has also been in and out of adult prison. His younger siblings are in care and he is regretful that he has not seen them for some time and says he would like to be a better role model to them.

> (I'd like to) get a place of our own, settle down and just get on with life and leave the past behind us. (Joe)

> Get my job back, get proper counselling, stay away from the drugs, and get back with me girlfriend. (Brendan)

For those not in a relationship the future was often linked to their families. Here a strong theme was repairing broken relationships.

> I know for a fact that there's a chance there. I know me ma will take me back. I just have to prove things to her, or else I'll get me own place, sort meself out, get a flat and start buying clothes and start going back to (name of district) to me proper friends. (David)

> I've four brothers and one sister and hopefully one day I'll be able to go back to them... Hopefully one day the whole family will get back together... I'll be happy when they're all older and meself older and I can settle down with me own kids and that, you know. I just want to give my kids the things I hadn't got. (Mark)

I want to try and get myself sorted before me dad dies,
I want him to see that I can do it, you know. (Barry)

For many participants with addiction problems their immediate goal was to become drug-free and therefore a promise of social housing or a methadone course was their objective. Many of those addicted to heroin were in poor health, which was an added difficulty.

Me dream, healthy first, get me health first. No drink,
no drugs, no methadone, no tablets, no nothing. I
want to feel good, you know what I mean, I want that.
That's what I want before a house, before a car, before
anything. (David)

Once I have a flat then I'll be laughing, that's all I
want, a flat, a job and to live a social life and go out
every Friday or Saturday night like everybody else
does. ..It wrecks my head, I'm sleeping in a doorway
on a Friday and Saturday night, you see everyone
going out, man, husband and wife, boyfriend,
girlfriend. And you're thinking to yourself, why
couldn't I be doing that, you know what I mean, and
that gives me all the more reason to say to myself:
"I'm getting out there and getting a job for meself",
you know what I mean. (Mark)

2.5 Conclusions

Each participant's story and pathway into homelessness is individual and reflects his specific personal history. However, several common themes and issues emerge from the case histories of these men.

❖ The participants did not follow the usual, graduated, pathways to independence, usually deviating from these routes at a very young age.

❖ A number of factors contributed to the men's difficulties in early childhood and youth. They were overwhelmingly from economically deprived backgrounds which limited resources and possibilities for the family. At a family level there was for many an absence of parenting either because a parent had left the family home or was unable to cope. These men lacked role models in their families and did not appear to have found a substitute figure outside the family. Many men grew up without a father in the home, or where the father was present and the relationship was often conflictual. Relationships with their mothers were generally more positive and supportive. Thus the family lives of the men were characterised by multiple traumas especially loss, disruption and instability.

❖ School was essentially a non-event for these men and did not present an opportunity to overcome previous negative events and experiences. The evidence is that they failed to engage with school, especially with second level schooling. This lack of educational skills was both cause and effect of developing allegiances to out of school interests and activities especially drug-taking. In terms of precipitants for leaving home drug taking and escape from difficult, abusive home situations predominated. Once out of home these men, unable to survive in the labour and housing markets and vulnerable to negative economic and personal events, slid into homelessness. Exiting from this state became difficult as their problems were compounded by their out of home life.

❖ Living and surviving as a homeless person is dependent on maintaining contacts and sources of support especially with partners and family. Those from intact families had an advantage here. For those from splintered families isolation was only avoided by developing friendships and support within the homeless system. Maintaining an identity was also key in the face of stigmatising encounters with the public and authorities. Avoiding further demoralisation and looking to the future optimistically and to the prospect of life with a home was also important.

What emerges from their narratives and this analysis is that a series of difficulties in their young lives – personal, familial, educational and structural – narrowed their life options as they grew to adulthood. They themselves further reduced their opportunities by engaging in drug use and anti-social behaviour. As Rutter (1989) and others have noted, this kind of background increases the possibility of future negative events and conversely reduces the chance of positive experiences.

But why is the homeless population so overwhelmingly male? To understand this one needs to address issues around masculinity and in particular disadvantaged masculinities. These men appear to conform to the profile of disadvantaged masculinities as presented by Hearn (1998) and others. As Mac an Ghaill (1994) has shown, some working class men continue to adhere to traditional norms of manhood although these are becoming increasingly outdated and the potential avenues for these forms of masculinities are decreasing. This offers, in part, an explanation of their social descent. But the compounding effects of family and personal problems, difficulties which these men experienced to a significant degree, are also very much part of the explanation.

Men's homelessness and marginalisation is connected with structural issues of poverty, with the effectiveness and level of the educational resources and support services for families and children they received, the ability to avail of these services and with personal issues embedded in their family experiences and with gender and masculinity factors. These issues are brought together in the final section of the report.

Linking the Contextual and Experiential Features of Marginalisation

3

3.1 Summary and Discussion

The first chapter of this report, the context of marginalisation amongst young men in Ireland examined the areas of the family, education and the economy as well as marginalized groupings and links between changing value systems and the alienation of young men. The second chapter focused on the lives and experiences of a group of homeless men in Dublin. In this final chapter an attempt is made to combine the main findings of both the contextual and experiential sections of the study.

Family factors

In the last three decades we have experienced change in both the structure and dynamics of the family in Ireland. More diverse family forms, including those headed by a woman only, are now common, although these represent a minority of family units. There is change but there are also continuities. The two-parent family remains predominant and men are still more likely to be the main breadwinner. However, more than half of all families do not rely on fathers as the exclusive breadwinner and many are now dependent on income earned by both parents and or state benefits. These changes have undoubtedly influenced men's lives.

Family transformations have challenged traditional values about the family, marriage and parenting roles. The balance of power within families has been affected by the movement of married women into the labour market. The fact that women now work outside the home implies alternative, non-home based, care for children from an early age, and, potentially, more egalitarian parental responsibilities for children. Women are less tied to the institution of marriage. They are now more likely to initiate a family unit on their own or to end a marital relationship. These developments have been aided by legal recognition of non-marital states and parenthood.

Fathers within families may be experiencing difficulties in the face of changing definitions of fatherhood in that work demands may operate against them in developing closer relationships with their children. Yet there are indications that men are adapting and welcoming change related to fatherhood and other roles. A majority of middle-class men now enter marriage accepting that their wife will probably work for most of their union and that they will both contribute to childcare and domestic duties. There is evidence of more flexibility around male roles and behaviour generally. Recognition of differing forms of masculinities, of different ways of being a man, is apparent and this has been incorporated to some extent into domestic and corporate spheres (Connell and Wood 2002). These developments have problematised traditional constructs of masculinity and some men now view adherence to a stereotypical masculinity as non-adaptive in contemporary life. But not all men have the resources readily available to accommodate change. Men who were in the past more likely to enter marriage are now less likely to avail of this option either because the mothers of their children are willing to accept the main responsibility for childrearing and or because they cannot contribute financially to the union. Overall, there is variation in male responses to change. Some men are negotiating different ways of relating to the world while others are feeling undermined because "the inherited script of masculinity" is no longer available (Owens 2000, p.52).

Changes within the family, discussed above, potentially affect all families and all children but the focus in this study is whether certain types of family are more likely to produce troubled boys and young men. The contention that children in families without a father per se are psychologically and socially damaged is, empirically, difficult to sustain. The key variables in all families appear to be the ability of the parent to parent and economic resources. When these features combine negatively, when there is a serious lack of parenting combined with disadvantage, then children in both lone and two-parent families, may be vulnerable. Lone parent families may be sites of additional risk for male children because they are more likely to be economically disadvantaged and because of the way young males sometimes respond to difficulties. Family discord appears to affect boys more than girls or at least males are more likely to show distress in an overt way thus alerting parents and teachers to their behaviour. Boys are more likely to be involved by parents in marital difficulties and to be the targets of parental hostility within families. The internal nature of female distress is less obvious and more 'socially acceptable' and thus the extent of this disturbance may not emerge until later in adolescence or adulthood.

Young boys are more likely to develop behavioural disorders and this is linked to a problematic family background but it is also connected to economic disadvantage. Such disorder does not usually persist into adulthood but disadvantaged young men who experience home and school difficulties are at risk of developing these conditions and of these difficulties continuing into adulthood. A compounding factor is often the boy's involvement in out-of-home (and school) sub-groups which may be linked to anti-social behaviour such as substance abuse. Whether males become embedded in this lifestyle is therefore dependent on personal, family, educational and economic factors as well as their geographical location. Particular neighbourhoods increase the likelihood of allegiance to deviant lifestyles. Yet, children and young people are not passive agents and, in general, actively negotiate their way through, and out of, family and other difficulties. It does appear however that the choices available to some children are restricted from an early age and their options become increasingly confined as they grow older.

A number of family-related risk features were evident in the study of homeless men. There were identifiable routes to homelessness and the trajectory started at a very early age, usually within the family unit. Factors such as inadequate parenting (due to alcoholism, substance abuse or other problems) were present and there was a good deal of violence in their young lives. This created both a feeling of powerlessness in the child as well as providing a model of behaviour in which violence is seen as a typical response mechanism. There was also an abundance of loss experiences in their family lives and for some men losses were recurring as they changed from one care situation to another. These events and experiences contribute to a pattern of disrupted attachments and this effect was identifiable in the men's narratives.

The sample is too small to infer any disadvantage from lone parenthood alone. Lone parenthood in this group usually resulted from separation, often following domestic violence, and the father was often present for part of the man's childhood. What did appear to be important was the residue of anger and resentment towards the father. As a consequence relationships with fathers were either non-existent or conflicted. There was uncertainty about male behaviour and the men lacked, by their own admission, a male role model. They also demonstrated ambivalence towards violence. Men who had witnessed and or experienced domestic violence as children found this abhorrent but were often, by their own admission, violent themselves. And, as their lives developed they were increasingly placed in environments where violence rather than conciliation was a more probable response.

Many children have experienced events and difficulties in their lives and have coped successfully but what is characteristic of these men's childhoods is multiple trauma in the context of economic disadvantage. The sample were overwhelmingly from economically deprived backgrounds which, along with the difficulties outlined above, supports the contextual evidence that disadvantage in the broad sense is strongly implicated in homelessness. In addition, they were, according to their own narratives, from neighbourhoods where social problems such as drug taking were widespread. This spatial aspect to disadvantage is recognised as related to young people's initiation into drug-taking cultures and this was clearly so for some of the participants.

There is an interesting insight from the men's stories and narrative into the contemporary position of men, in particular lone fathers. The participants all viewed relationships and fatherhood as important and stabilising features in their lives and the majority expressed a desire for a long term bond or marriage. Yet the present social and economic status of the men, and, in particular, the stories of those who were fathers, suggests that stable relationships are unlikely for these men. Having a child is no longer a route into such a relationship. They were aware of this, as they were conscious of the powerful position of women, relative to them, in respect of parenthood. Not having a home or even a private place in which to meet with your child adds a particularly testing dimension to being a father.

Education
There is increasing evidence of a female predominance in the Irish education system, and this reflects findings from other countries. Males appear, from overall figures, to be less successful than females at all levels and within all educational sectors. But not all male students are doing equally badly and some are doing exceptionally well. A key factor in explaining differential male achievement and underachievement from primary level upwards is socio-economic status and this is underplayed in some analysis of

educational trends. Another possibility is that the extent of the gender differential has been exaggerated with findings based on a less than comprehensive array of assessments. Boys may simply appear to be underachieving because girls are now performing better. Females, more so than males, have reacted positively to increasing educational and occupational opportunities and males may have yielded what was once their natural advantage.

The key question in this discussion is why male children and young men from lower socio-economic groupings are more likely than others to underachieve and or opt out of the educational system altogether? The reasons may be personal, familial, pedagogical or socio-economic. Disengagement may occur because of the incompatibility of the, largely middle class, school system with the child's socio-cultural background. There may be fewer resources available to such children in their schools but this is only one possible contributory factor to underachievement. The more important site in relation to educational success is probably the child's home, specifically parental attitudes to education. Another factor inhibiting educational success may be learning difficulties especially if there are insufficient resources and skills available to help the child. Boys exhibit more specific attention and learning difficulties than girls and these conditions sometimes co-exist alongside behavioural disorder. These factors together create vulnerability for involvement in deviant behaviour. That learning difficulties are a contributory factor to exclusion is evidenced by the high prevalence of such problems amongst marginalized groupings such as the homeless and offenders. It is also evident from the stories of men who returned to education in adulthood to redress literacy difficulties. These narratives chart unhappy and alienating school experiences and attempts to regain control by projecting an indifference to one's plight thus causing further disengagment from the system. And most especially, there is, in these men's stories, a profound sense of shame which is concealed into adulthood behind the detached persona of traditional masculinity. This lack of schooling had a significant effect on their life chances. An educational deficiency places people, in general, in a disadvantaged position but when this occurs in the midst of rising educational expectations there are likely to be more profound consequences. As educational skills provide entrée to a wide range of reflexive and communicative abilities which assist survival in a rapidly changing society, those without these skills are placed at a severe disadvantage. The empowering aspect of education as well as the implications of schooling deficits, is evident in the words of an early school leaver who later returned to education:

> *Education changed me and I would like to see that change happen for all working-class men. Because if that change doesn't happen a lot of guys are going to stay long-term unemployed, isolated, frustrated, get angry, violent,...if they don't reach some sort of personal view of themselves that is warm or humane, we're going to have a lot of problems with lads. And I think it's going to get worse* (Owens 2000, p.23).

Young men from working class backgrounds may leave school early due to what has been referred to as an antagonism between educational attainment and the achievement of traditional and valued masculinities. Both the ethos and learning format of formal schooling may be more suitable for some children than others and males who are doing less well will take steps to avoid any potential humiliation. There are various means of resistance available in schools and one such method is to adopt an exaggerated masculinity in direct contrast to that masculinity which fits into the system. As with family and other difficulties experienced, children actively select and evaluate knowledge and opportunities around education. Young men from this background may therefore seek more secure sources of self-esteem in out-of-school groupings if school does not prove to be a site for success and self-enhancement. But transitions to work and independence become more risk-laden without educational qualifications. Not every male who drops out of school is on the pathway to dependence and marginalisation but there is a higher probability of this happening if this is compounded by other risk factors.

A deficit of educational skills was obvious amongst the homeless men interviewed for this study. There was a failure on their part to engage with both the structure and the experience of school and this became more marked for the participants as they moved into secondary school. Two elements were probably instrumental in channelling these men away from school. Firstly, both behavioural and or specific learning difficulties were apparent in the group from an early age and this would have made academic success increasingly difficult as they moved through the system. And some of the participants were aware that they had problems with learning which required help. Secondly the clustering of adversity in their family lives would have compounded their academic problems. This combination of difficulties would also have increased the likelihood of their attaching to others in similar positions, especially if there were reference groups available in the neighbourhood. According to some of the participants they left school because they found out-of-school activities more attractive or because they had become involved in drug-taking.

For these men, to break out of the cycle of disadvantage, from which the majority had emerged, would have required particular skills and motivation in school and or positive attitudes from parents or significant other/s. None of these resources were available to them and in reality school failed to make any real impact on these men's lives. The series of disadvantages - personal, economic and familial - these men experienced, and the fact they appeared to happen simultaneously during their childhood, is crucial in understanding their life pathways. The lack of educational and vocational skills militated against them in trying to gain independence as it is now preventing them from moving out of homelessness.

Work

Men's identities have traditionally been formed partly through the predominance of certain kinds of jobs and occupations. The decline of long-established male work areas alongside the rise of job sectors accessible to both men and women has changed the labour market in Ireland and elsewhere. Negotiation of the job market requires new skills and educational resources as well as personal confidence. Changes in the labour market which have impacted on male roles in the workplace and in the family have been referred to above as well as the fact that these changes may have had more serious consequences for some men than others.

Males from lower socio-economic backgrounds are much more likely to have low levels of educational attainment and vocational training than females or other Irish males. This has important implications for their chances of success in the labour market and these young men are doing significantly less well than men from higher socio-economic backgrounds. Similarly, some men are holding on to increasingly obsolete forms of masculinity although there is a less prospect of finding 'masculine type' work and this type of work is more susceptible to economic fluctuations. Disadvantage and poverty decreases still further one's chances of compensating for lost skills and these features tend to cluster in specific districts. Females from working class backgrounds are doing somewhat better than males from similar environments in accessing further education and employment. They also have entrée to a more 'socially acceptable' alternative to education and employment – early motherhood.

Educational deficits led to problems gaining and retaining employment for the homeless men interviewed in this study. This seriously affected their chances of making a successful transition from home to independent living. Their employment prospects are now exacerbated by lack of familiarity with the world of work as well as, in many cases, by health and substance abuse problems. The lack of a home, and not having a 'proper address', also hampered their chances of finding work. There are also financial disincentives to paid work at this level. Consequently, very few of these men had had a job of any significant length and most had not worked at all in the recent past. The majority, in common with the long-term unemployed generally, have now become disengaged from the labour market despite their relative youth.

Involvement in marginalised lifestyles

There are similarities between men who feature in different marginalized categories. These include deprivation in their background, a history of educational and learning deficits and a lack of economic resources, job skills and experience.

The connection between homelessness and disadvantage is apparent from studies of the homeless population. Problematic family histories are common as is being raised in care settings. There are also links to substance abuse and alcoholism. Amongst homeless men the problem of educational and economic marginalisation are magnified. These men are less well educated (they are often early school leavers) and vocationally trained than the general population of men. They have usually been out of work for some years – casual work in the past giving way to a complete cessation of work. Their economic and educational difficulties are generally compounded by personal and health problems and they are sometimes involved in petty crime, usually to fund a drug habit.

There is a comparable association between offenders and socio-economic background. Men predominate in crime statistics but young, working class men are over-represented amongst offenders. Recorded crime is also associated with specific geographical areas. This is true in Ireland and elsewhere although the link between crime and lower socio-economic status could be a feature of the way crime is defined and detected. The social class differential in crime statistics might be explained as the response of these young men to social and economic exclusion. That disadvantaged young men are particularly sensitive to their position in an environment of affluence is apparent from various research sources. The male predominance in crime could also be viewed as an outlet for traditional and often violent manifestations of masculinity to emerge.

The link between drug use, which is predominantly a male activity and crime is evident from the data presented in chapters one and two of this study. Drug use is predominantly a male activity and begins at a young age, usually during adolescence. Drug users and offenders exhibit a particularly low level of education and vocational skills and they frequently drop out of school before the required leaving age. They are typically from lower socio-economic backgrounds and both groups cluster in specific geographical, primarily disadvantaged, areas. The majority of drug users have a criminal record, usually involving relatively minor crime, the type of crime necessary to maintain a drug habit.

In the case study the intertwining of homelessness, drugs and crime are apparent. Some men became homeless as a direct or indirect effect of drugs. Others began to take drugs or advanced to more serious forms of drug-taking when they were homeless. Crime, usually of a minor kind, was used to maintain a drug habit and was generally not evident in the profiles of non-drug users. For those who were addicted, drugs were viewed as a major stumbling block in preventing them from leaving homelessness and moving on in their lives.

Change, integration and psychological alienation

The pattern of rapid social change experienced in Ireland since the 1970s and the concurrent rise in the male suicide rate has led to attempts to link the two phenomena. The association, it is proposed, might be related to the lessening importance of religion and the development of a more individualist, secular, society. Young people have, in general, rejected the moral teachings of the Catholic Church and demonstrate more of the liberal values indicative of a secular, individualist society than older age cohorts. Yet there is no pattern of widespread alienation as young people continue to support a communal ethos and general levels of happiness appear to be stable across age groupings. However, there is an increased acceptance of suicide especially among young men. Increased tolerance for suicide is associated with economic growth and individualism and each of these factors is correlated with rising suicide rates in most countries. The juxtaposition of improving social conditions with escalating suicide levels might be interpreted as indicative of a general alienation among young males or, alternatively, as reflecting the social exclusion of some specific groupings of males.

The rise in young male, but not female, suicide prompts the question why young men rather than young women have been affected in this way? Explanations for this have centred on traditional male roles and behaviours, in particular their lack of access to confiding networks and their inability to disclose distress as well as the lethality of the methods used by men. Analysis of economic data have provided some interesting results, in particular, the strong correlation between a rising male suicide rate and the movement of married women into the labour market. This and other elements of social change in Ireland may have resulted in a reduction in male protective features - at-home spouse and stability in the educational and labour sectors. Additionally, in Ireland the ideological basis to male authority within the family and the community is no longer as influential. Women, conversely, may have benefited more than men from social transformations in this country. They have achieved greater equality in the home and the job market and while they have developed a substantial degree of independence from the organisational Church, they have retained a greater degree of spiritual belief than men. The latter factor seems to be protective in terms of mental health and suicide.

Social change, economic, educational, gender and religious change, may all have contributed in various, but complex, ways to the rise in male suicide in Ireland. It is unlikely that there is a single explanation as to why people end their lives but there are identifiable themes. Broad societal factors form a normative backdrop from which people draw ideas about behaviour. That this backdrop is increasingly international rather than culture-specific is obvious from the similarity of international patterns of youth suicide. Thus if suicide becomes more acceptable in a society there is greater likelihood than in the past that this form of behaviour will be resorted to if a person is confronted with difficulties. Personal and societal transition creates vulnerability. Thus adolescents and young adults face additional challenges in the midst of social transformation. In Ireland as well as other European countries women have been experiencing a period of incremental gains while men have found their traditional ways of being and behaving challenged. Yet as the foregoing analysis has shown men, perhaps even the majority of men, are adapting and welcoming some of these changes particularly closer relationships with their children. But some men may be more alienated and thus more at risk of suicide.

The social transformations discussed in this report have benefited and empowered many sections of the population but they probably have also isolated those not carried along with this change. Some, mainly working class men, are doing less well educationally and economically and it is here that the links between personal, economic and psychological factors come together. The possibility that educational deficits may be linked to an adherence to outmoded masculine routes and behaviours has been addressed above. Education has become an important signifier of achievement and not being successful educationally, and thus jobwise, must, conversely, bring with it some notions of failure. Men who engage in suicidal behaviour are less likely to have the social and other benefits of education and are more likely to lack economic resources. They are unlikely to be involved in relationships and to have little possibility of developing stable partnerships in the future. They are risk laden in an era of flux and impermanence. They may also be confined by the limitations of traditional masculinity and are unlikely to disclose distress. These experiences are exemplified in the marginalized groupings considered in this report.

The homeless men interviewed in this study reflect these risk features for psychological alienation. In personal, economic and social terms these men were isolated and marginalized. They felt excluded from the usual social networks and they were acutely conscious of their status outside of society. There were aware of the benefits of stable, confiding relationships yet they knew that their present situation militated against their forming a family unit even if they had children. Faced with the fragility of sexual relationships their sense of family centred on their children. They wanted to form closer bonds with them but they had access to almost none of the practical necessities for meeting and communicating with their children. The benefits of fatherhood were therefore somewhat lost to them as they were to their children. Economic exclusion had resulted in marginalization from fatherhood and family life.

The men attempted to maintain social relationships within the homeless community but it was clear from their narratives that these contacts lacked depth and trust. Their attempts to sustain links with others and to look optimistically to the future were not always successful. Loneliness and despair were evident amongst some of the participants and this was affecting their well-being and mental health. The men were not asked directly about suicidal behaviour but the topic arose spontaneously in some of the interviews. It is clear from at least one man's story that suicidal action was resorted to when relationship bonds were threatened.

3.2 Conclusions

Despite widespread change in masculine roles the evidence is that the majority of men are adjusting and adapting to change. Women are now in the majority in upper levels of educational achievement. Males are still well represented at these levels and some young men are outperforming females in examinations and at postgraduate level.

There is improved access to, and more equality in, the labour market but there is no evidence that women are moving to a position of dominance across employment sectors. Married women's working has had consequences in the home but again there is evidence of adaptation and even an appreciation by men of new parental responsibilities.

Greater flexibility around definitions of masculinities may also have aided men in developing new roles and behaviours. There is, as Connell and Wood (2002) have said, no general crisis of masculinity. The social transformation of the last three decades may have led to "frayed understandings of what it means to be a man" (Haywood and Mac an Ghaill 2003) but this change is part of wider developments affecting both men and women. These gender changes have produced responses from men ranging from role re-orientation to confusion to anger and rejection.

In today's society, plural rather than unitary identities are to the fore and those who can accumulate identity enhancing resources have a better chance of maintaining psychological equilibrium. Conversely those who accumulate risks in an uncertain socio-environment will be vulnerable. Some categories of men, mainly young, working class men, have found these social and economic transformations difficult because they are confined by their gender and world view. Males from these backgrounds are more likely to miss out on the benefits of school which results in job instability and an inability to set up an independent life. They are also more likely to be members of marginalized groupings such as the homeless. The main task of this report was to establish the origins and trajectory for these lifestyles.

There is no empirical evidence that lone (female) parent families per se are more likely to produce problematic males. This risk is more connected to economic disadvantage. Male children can overcome the loss of a father if they can access other models for behaviour. They can also develop beneficial relationships with out-of-home fathers as the diversity of fatherhood becomes increasingly common. What may be difficult for boys in these circumstances is if their relationship with their father is problematic and or the father provides models of disempowering rather than empowering behaviour. If family difficulties contribute to making school problematic for a child, any degree of learning difficulties will exacerbate the situation. If school then fails to provide a positive route out of the family, the boy is more likely to drop out of school and fall under the influence of out-of-school cultures. In some urban areas such cultures often involve drug-taking. The explanation for boy's greater tendency for overtly deviant behaviour as they develop may be explained in terms of a greater propensity amongst males to externalise problems from an early age and the greater probability that these difficulties will come to the attention of school and specialist services. It is apparent that the majority of young men in Ireland do not follow such a route. Yet some young men do follow this trajectory and it appears that early problems are more likely to cluster in socially deprived male groupings.

The men whose stories are presented here are all different but similar themes run through their lives. What emerges from their narratives and this analysis is that a series of difficulties in their young lives – personal, familial and educational – narrowed their life options as they grew to adulthood. Some of the men had been separated from home, school and other systems from an early age. This was often due to a problematic home background and parenting difficulties. Many had conflicting relationships with their fathers. Although some of this group did have other family members who provided assistance, the absence of consistent, alternative sources of care and self-esteem, appeared to be a crucial deficit. If familial problems become connected to school difficulties it increases the possibility of marginalisation from the usual routes. Learning difficulties, not being able to avail of schooling, increases the likelihood of opting out of school.

A number of common themes have emerged from both the documentary analysis and the interviews with homeless men. There are clear similarities in the backgrounds of different marginalised groupings. Poor levels of education, followed by little or no vocational training, a lack of success in the job market and a background of personal, familial and health difficulties appear to be common features. Structural features, especially poverty, are also important. Problematic home backgrounds in many cases created an initial risk element. The education process offers the possibility to redress family based difficulties but it may be difficult if not impossible for some children to avail of this. Students are failing and disengaging from the system for a variety of reasons and these factors are usually in place from a very early age. If a child's problem is not addressed, and many of the homeless men in this study were aware that their early problems were not dealt with, then the boy's difficulties are more likely to be manifested in a behavioural, conduct disordered, way. The pathway may then be set for a problematic school career with the consequent work and other difficulties outlined in this report.

Social and psychological integration are probably linked, albeit in complex ways, to suicidal behaviour. Suicide is more acceptable generally as a behaviour option. Marginalised male groupings (the homeless, offenders and those who abuse drugs) have a high level of suicidal behaviour and it is empirically as well as intuitively obvious that marginalisation and its consequences are likely to be internalised. This, along with frequent assaults on one's identity

130

and the need to maintain a will to survive in very difficult circumstances, makes it more likely that suicide could become an option for these men. Male predominance in these groups, as well as other isolated categories (such as single rural men) contributes to male over-representation in suicide statistics.

The conclusion of this report is that despite challenge and confusion amongst men there is no general crisis of masculinity. What is evident is the increasing isolation and alienation of a particular grouping of men who are in this situation due to a combination of structural, familial and personal factors. Certain categories of boys and young men are an at risk group in terms of personal development, education and economic factors. These deficits are apparent very early in their lives. The temptation may be to ignore the (relatively small) group identified as vulnerable in this report, when most children and young people are doing well. A solution would require a concerted and comprehensive approach. Perhaps the failure of some past initiatives is related to the fragmentation of education, family support, employment and health initiatives, and the fact that these interventions may not have been introduced early enough in the child's life.

Bibliography

Allen, G. (Ed.) (1999), *The Sociology of the Family*. Oxford: Blackwell.

Annandale, E. (1998), *The Sociology of Health and Medicine*. Cambridge: Polity Press.

An Garda Síochána, *Annual Report 1999*. Dublin: Government Publications Office.

Barber, J.G. (2001), 'Relative Misery and Youth Suicide'. *Australian and New Zealand Journal of Psychiatry*: 35, 49-57.

Beardslee, W.R. and D. Podorefsky (1988), 'Resilient Adolescents whose Parents have Serious Affective and other Psychiatric Disorders: Importance of Self-Understanding and Relationships'. *American Journal of Psychiatry*: 145, 63-69.

Beck, U. and E. Beck-Gernsheim. (2002), *The Normal Chaos of Love*. Cambridge, UK: Polity Press.

Beck, U. (1992), *The Risk Society*. London: Sage.

Bernstein, B. (1971), *Class, Codes and Control*, Vol. 1. London: Routledge and Kegan Paul.

Bille-Brahe, U., K. Andersen, D. Wasserman, A. Schmidtke, T. Bjerke, P. Crepet, D. de Leo, C. Haring, K. Hawton, A. Kerkhof, J. Lönnqvist, K. Michel, A. Phillipe, I. Querejeta, E. Salander-Renberg and B. Temesváry, (1996). 'The WHO/EURO Multicentre Study: Risk of Parasuicide and the Comparability of the Areas under Study'. *Crisis* 17(1), 32-42.

Bourdieu, P. and J.C. Passeron. (1977), *Reproduction of Education, Society and Culture*. London: Sage.

Breault, K.D. (1986), 'Suicide in America: a Test of Durkheim's Theory of Religious and Family Integration' 1933-1980. American Journal of Sociology, 92: 628-656.

Breen, M. (2002), 'Different from their Elders and Betters: Age Cohort Differences in the Irish Data of the European Values Study (EVS) 1999' in Cassidy, E.G. Measuring Ireland: Discerning Values and Beliefs. Dublin: Veritas Publications.

Breslin, A. and J. Weafer. (1985), Religious Beliefs, Practice and Moral Attitudes: A Comparison of Two Irish Surveys 1974-1984. Maynooth: Council for Research and Development.

Brody, H. (1982), Inishkillane: Change and Decline in the West of Ireland. London: Jill Norman and Hobhouse: London.

Browne, C., A, Daly and D. Walsh. (2000), Irish Psychiatric Services Activities 1998. Dublin: Health Research Board.

Callan, T., C. O'Neill and C. O'Donoghue. (1995), Supplementing Family Incomes. Policy Research Series Paper No. 23, Dublin: Economic and Social Research Institute.

Callan, T., B. Nolan, B.J. Whelan, C.T. Whelan and J. Williams. (1996), Poverty in the 1990s: Evidence from the Living in Ireland Survey. General Research Series, Paper No. 170. Dublin: Oak Tree Press/Combat Poverty Agency.

Canetto, S.S. (1997), 'Meanings of Gender and Suicidal Behavior during Adolescence'. Suicide and Life Threatening Behaviour, 27(4), 339-351.

Carroll, E. (2002), 'Indicators of Child Well-being: Exploring Conceptual Measurement Issues' in Cassidy, E.G. Measuring Ireland: Discerning Values and Beliefs. Dublin: Veritas Publications.

Cassidy, E.G. (2002), 'Modernity and Religion in Ireland 1980-2000' in Cassidy, E.G. Measuring Ireland: Discerning Values and Beliefs. Dublin: Veritas Publications.

Chambers, D. (1999), *National Suicide Review Group Annual Report.* Galway: Western Health Board.

Clancy, P. (2001), *College Entry in Focus: A Fourth National Survey of Access to Higher Education.* Dublin: Higher Education Authority.

Clancy, P. (1982), 'Does School Type Matter – the Unresolved Questions'. *Sociological Association of Ireland Bulletin,* 45: 12-14.

Clancy, P. (1987), *Participation in Higher Education.* Dublin: Higher Education Authority.

Clancy, P. (1988), *Who Goes to College*? Dublin: Higher Education Authority.

Clancy, P. (1995), *Access to College: Patterns of Continuity and Change,* Dublin: Higher Education Authority.

Clancy, P. and J. Wall. (2000), *Social Background of Higher Education Entrants.* Dublin: Higher Education Authority.

Clare, A. (2000), *On Men: Masculinity and Crisis.* London: Chatto and Windus.

Cleary, A. (1997a), 'Gender and Mental Health' in Cleary, A and Treacy, M. *The Sociology of Health and Illness in Ireland.* Dublin: UCD Press.

Cleary, A. (1997b), 'Madness and Mental Health in Irish Women' in Berne, A. and M. Leonard (Eds.) *Women and Irish Society: A Sociological Reader* (pp 233-250). Belfast: Beyond the Pale Productions.

Cleary, A, E. Nixon and M. Fitzgerald. (2004), *From Childhood to Adult: A Longitudinal Study of Children and their Families.* Report commissioned by the Department of Social, Community and Family Affairs. (Expected publication date: April 2004).

Cleary, A. and Prizeman, G. (1999), *Homelessness and Mental Health.* Dublin: Combat Poverty/ Homelessness and Mental Health Action Group.

134

Cleary, A., M. Nic Ghiolla Phádraig and S. Quin. (2001) *Understanding Children. Volume 1: State, Education and Economy.* Dublin: Oak Tree Press.

Cleary, A., M. Nic Ghiolla Phádraig and S. Quin. (2001) *Understanding Children. Volume 2: Changing Experiences and Family Forms.* Dublin: Oak Tree Press.

Connell, R.W. (1989), 'Cool Guys, Swots and Wimps: the Inter-play of Masculinity and Education'. *Oxford Review of Education*, 15(3):291-303.

Connell, R.W. (1995), *Masculinities.* Cambridge: Polity Press.

Connell, R.W. and J. Wood (2002), *Globalisation and Business Masculinities'.* Paper delivered in Trinity College Dublin in November 2002 , part of a serious of lectures on masculinities organised by the Department of Education and Science (Equality Section).

Connolly, J.F. and D. Lester. (2000), 'Suicide Rates in Irish Counties'. *Irish Journal of Psychological Medicine, 17 (2):59-61.*

Corcoran, P., M.J. Kelleher, H.S. Keeley, S. Berne, U. Burke and E. Williamson. (1997), 'A Preliminary Statistical Model for Identifying Repeaters of Parasuicide.' *Archives of Suicide Research.* 3: 65-74.

Corridan, M. (2002), *Moving from the Margins.* Dublin: Dublin Adult Learning Centre.

Council for Research and Development (2000). *Religious Beliefs and Practice: A New Survey.* Maynooth: St. Patrick's College.

Council for Research and Development (1998), *Attitudes to the Catholic Church: Comment on R.T.E.Primetime/M.R.B.I survey.* Maynooth: St. Patrick's College.

Cross, S.E. and L. Madson. (1997), 'Models of the Self: Self-construal and Gender'. *Psychological Bulletin*, 122(1):5-37.

Central Statistics Office, (CSO) (various years), Census of Population, *Household Composition and Family Units.* Dublin: Stationery Office.

CSO (various years), Census of Population, *Principal Demographic Results*. Dublin: Stationery Office.

CSO (various years), Census of Population, *Population Classified by Area*. Dublin: Stationery Office.

CSO (various years), Census of Population, *Ages and Marital Status*. Dublin: Stationery Office.

CSO (1996), Census of Population, *Principal Socio-economic Results*. Dublin: Stationery Office.

CSO (1996), Census of Population, *Industries and Occupations*. Dublin: Stationery Office.

CSO, (2000) Statistical Release, *Quarterly National Household Survey*. Dublin: Stationery Office.

CSO, (2003) *Quarterly National Household Survey*. (First Quarter 2003). Dublin: Stationery Office.

CSO, (various years) *Labour Force Surveys*. Dublin: Stationery Office.

CSO, (various years) *Vital Statistics*. Dublin: Stationery Office.

CSO, (1997), Statistical Release, *Women in the Workforce*. Dublin: Stationery Office.

CSO (2000), *"That was Then, This is Now" Change in Ireland, 1949-1999*. Dublin: Stationery Office.

Department of Education and Science. The *Economic Status of School Leavers: Results of School Leavers' Surveys* 1994-1999. Dublin: Stationery Office.

Department of Education and Science (2000), *Learning for Life: White Paper on Adult Education*. Dublin: Stationery Office.

Department of Education and Science (2000), *Educational Initiatives to Combat Disadvantage*. Dublin: Stationery Office.

Department of Health and Children (1998) Report *of the National Task Force on Suicide.* Dublin: Stationery Office.

Departments of Public Health (2001). *Suicide in Ireland: A National Study.* Published by the Departments of Public Health on behalf of the Chief Executive Officers of the Health Boards.

Department of Social Community and Family Affairs (various years), *Statistical Report on Social Welfare Services.* Sligo: DSCFA

Department of Social Community and Family Affairs/Commission on the Family, (1998), *Strengthening Families for Life, Final Report to the Minister for Social Community and Family Affairs.* Dublin: Stationery Office.

Dillon, L. (2001). *Drug Use Among Prisoners: An Exploratory Study.* Dublin: Health Research Board.

Doody, B. (2000) *Unpublished Data/ Personal Communication.*

Drudy, S. and K. Lynch. (1993), *Schools and Society in Ireland.* Dublin: Gill and Macmillan. Dublin.

Duncombe, J. and D. Marsden. (1993), 'Love and Intimacy: The Gender Division of Emotion and Emotion Work.' *Sociology,* 27 (2): 221-241.

Durkheim, E. (1951), *Suicide: A Study in Sociology* (Translated by R. Spaulding). London: Routledge and Kegan Paul.

Eckersley, R. (2001), 'Culture, Health and Well-being' in: Eckersley, R, J. Dixon and J. Douglas, *The Social Origins of Health and Well-being.* Melbourne: Cambridge University Press.

Eckersley, R. and K. Dear. (2002), 'Cultural Correlates of Youth Suicide'. *Social Science and Medicine,* 55: 891-1904.

Economic and Social Research Institute (1998), *Annual School Leavers Survey.* Dublin: Economic and Social Research Institute.

Fahey, T. (2002), 'Is Atheism Increasing? Ireland and Europe Compared' in Cassidy, E.G. *Measuring Ireland: Discerning Values and Beliefs.* Dublin: Veritas Publications.

Fahey, T. and D. Watson. (1995), *An Analysis of Social Housing Need.* General Research Series, Paper No. 168. Dublin: Economic and Social Research Institute.

Fahey, T. and H. Russell (2001), *Family Formation in Ireland: Trends, Data Needs and Implications.* Dublin: Economic and Social Research Institute.

Farrell, Warren. (1994), *The Myth of Male Power: Why Men are the Disposable Sex.* London: Fourth Estate,   .

Feeney, A., H. McGee, T. Holohan and W. Shannon. (2000), *Health of Hostel-Dwelling Men in Dublin.* Dublin: Royal College of Surgeons/Eastern Health Board.

Fergusson, D. and L. Horwood. (1998), 'Early Conduct Problems and Later Life Opportunities'. *Journal of Emotional and Behavioural Disorders,* 6, 2-18.

Fergusson, D. and M. Lynskey. (1998), 'Conduct Problems in Childhood and Psychosocial Outcomes in Young Adulthood: A Prospective Study'. *Journal of Emotional and Behavioural Disorders,* 6:2-18.

Fitzgerald, E., B. Ingolsbe and F. Daly. (2000), *Solving Long-Term Unemployment in Dublin.* Dublin: Dublin Employment Pact, Policy Paper No. 2.

Fitzgerald, M. and A. Jeffers. (1994), 'Psychological Factors Associated with Psychological Problems in Irish Children and their Mothers'. *The Economic and Social Review,* 25 (4): 285-301.

Flanagan, N. (2001). 'Single Mothers and Parenting Outcomes' in Cleary, A., M. Nic Ghiolla Phádraig and S. Quin. (2001), *Understanding Children. Volume 2: Changing Experiences and Family Forms.* Dublin: Oak Tree Press.

Furstenburg, F.F. (1991), *Divided Families: What Happens to Children When Parents Part.* Cambridge MA: Harvard University Press.

Gamma/Trutz Haase (1999). *Affluence and Deprivation: A Spatial Analysis Based on the 1996 Census of Population.* Dublin: Gamma.

Garmezy, N. (1987), 'Stress, Competence and Development: Continuities in the Study of Schizophrenic Adults, Children Vulnerable to Psychopathology, and the Search for Stress-resistant Children'. *American Journal of Orthopsychiatry*, 57:159-174.

Geoghegan, T., M. O'Shea and G. Cox. (1999), 'Gender Differences in Characteristics of Drug Users Presenting to a Dublin Syringe Exchange'. *Psychological Medicine*, 16, 4.

Gilligan, R. (1993), 'Adversity in the Child's Home: The Protective Role of the Teacher and the School'. *Studies in Education*, 9:53-66.

Graham, H. (2000), *Introducing Phase 2 of the Programme, Health Variations*, Lancaster University: Economic and Social Research Council.

Greeley, A. (1994), 'Are the Irish Really Losing the Faith?'. *Doctrine and Life*, 44: 132-142.

Grotberg, E. (1995), *The International Resilience Project: Promoting Resilience in Children.* United States: ERIC Document Reproduction Service No. ED 383424.

Hanafin, J. (2000), Drover and Cloner: *The Agency of Intelligence in Structuring Sameness and Educational Exclusion.* Paper presented to the 27th Annual Conference of the Sociology Association of Ireland. *Ireland in the Twenty-First Century: Ideology, Power and Change.* Kilkenny, May 2000.

Hannan, D. and M. Boyle. (1987), *Schooling Decision: The Origins and Consequences of Selection and Streaming in Irish Post-Primary Schools.* Dublin: Economic and Social Research Institute.

Hannan, D. and S. Ó Riain. (1993), *Pathways to Adulthood in Ireland: Causes and Consequences of Success and Failure in Transitions amongst Irish Youth.* Dublin: Economic and Social Research Institute.

Harris, I. (1995), *Messages Men Hear: Constructing Masculinities.* London: Taylor & Francis.

Hayes, N. and M. Kernan. (2001), *Seven Years Old: School Experience in Ireland.* Dublin: Centre for Social and Educational Research, Dublin Institute of Technology.

Haywood, C. and M. Mac an Ghaill. (1997), ' A Man in the Making: Sexual Masculinities within Changing Training Cultures'. *The Sociological Review,* 45 (4): 576-588.

Haywood, C. and M. Mac an Ghaill (2003), *Men and Masculinities.* Buckingham, U.K.: Open University Press.

Hearn, J. (1998),' Troubled Masculinities in Social Policy Discourses: Young Men' in Popay J., J. Hearn and J. Edwards. (eds). *Men, Gender Divisions and Welfare.* London Routledge.

Hennessy, E. (2001) 'Children's Experiences in After-school Care' in Cleary, A., M. Nic Ghiolla Phádraig and S. Quin. (2001) *Understanding Children. Volume 2: Changing Experiences and Family Forms.* Dublin, Oak Tree Press.

Hetherington, E.M. ,M. Cox and R. Cox. (1982), 'Effects of Divorce on Parents and Children' in M. Lamb (Ed.) *Non Traditional Families.* Hillsdale NJ: Lawrence Erlbaum.

Hill, M. and K. Tisdall. (1997), *Children and Society.* Essex UK: Addison Wesley Longman Limited.

Hobcraft, J. and K. Kiernan (2001), 'Childhood Poverty, Early Motherhood and Adult Social Exclusion'. *British Journal of Sociology,* 52:495-517.

Hochschild, A. (1995), 'Understanding the Future of Fatherhood' in M. Van Dongan, G. Frinking and M. Jacobs (Eds.) *Changing Fatherhood*. Amsterdam: Thesis Publishers.

Holohan, T. (1997), *Health Status, Health Service Utilisation and Barriers to Health Service Utilisation among the Adult Homeless Population of Dublin*. Dublin: Eastern Health Board.

Hornsby-Smith, M.P. and Whelan. C.T. (1994), Religious and moral values in: C.T. Whelan (Ed) Values and Social Change in Ireland (page 7-44). Dublin: Gill and Macmillan.

Horwitz, A.L., C.S. Widom, J. McLoughlin and H.R. White (2001), 'Impact of Childhood Abuse and Neglect on Adult Mental Health: A Prospective Study.'. *Journal of Health and Social Behaviour*, 42:184-201.

Inglis, T. (1998), *Moral Monopoly: the Rise and Fall of the Catholic Church in Modern Ireland*, 2nd ed. Dublin: University College Dublin Press.

Inglis, T. (2002), 'Searching for Truth, Revealing Power, Hoping for Freedom' in Cassidy, E.G. *Measuring Ireland: Discerning Values and Beliefs*. Dublin: Veritas Publications.

International Social Survey Programme (1991, 1998), University College Dublin, unpublished data.

Irish Marketing Surveys (1999), *Religious Confidence Survey*. Dublin: Irish Marketing Surveys.

Irish Times. 28th February, 2003, 'Leaving Cert Numbers to Fall by 16,000'. *Report on proceedings of Oireachtas Committee on Education.*

Katz, A., A. Buchanan and A. McCoy. (2000), *Leading Lads: 1,400 lads Reveal What They Really Think about Life in Britain Today*. East Molesley, Durrey: Young Voice.

Keeley, H.S., P. Corcoran, A.M. Hennessy and M. Lawlor. (1999), *Background Stressors in Irish Parasuicides*. Poster presented at

Conference of the American Association of Suicidology, 14-18 April 1999, Houston, Texas.

Keeley, H.S. and M.J. Kelleher. (1998), *Youth Attitudes to Services in Ireland.* Psychiatric Bulletin 22(4): 257.

Kelleher, M.J. (1998a), *Youth Suicide Trends in the Republic of Ireland.* Br. J. Psychiatry, 173: 196-197.

Kelleher, M.J. (1998b), 'Suicide in Schools' in: Farrell B. (ed) *Issues in Education: Changing Education, Changing Society.* Dublin: Association of Secondary Teachers Ireland.

Kelleher, M.J., B. Keohane, C. Daly, H.S. Keeley, P. Corcoran, D. Chambers and E. Williamson. (1996), 'Deliberate Self-poisoning, Unemployment, and Public Health.' *Suicide and Life Threatening Behaviour,* 26(4):365-373.

Kelleher, M.J., D.Chambers and P. Corcoran. (1999), 'Suicide and Religion in Ireland: An Investigation of Thomas Masaryk's Theory of Suicide.' *Archives of Suicide Research,* 5: 173-180.

Kelleher, M.J., B. Keohane, C. Daly, H.S. Keeley, P. Corcoran, D. Chambers and E. Williamson. (1999), 'Individual Characteristics and Long-term Outcome for Deliberate Self-poisoners'. *Journal of the Irish College of Physicians and Surgeons,* 28(1): 5-8.

Kelleher, M.J. and M. Daly. (1990) 'Suicide in Cork and Ireland'. *British Journal of Psychiatry,* 157: 533-538.

Kelleher, P., C. Kelleher and M. Corbett (2000), *Left Out on Their Own: Young People Leaving Care in Ireland.* Dublin: Oak Tree Press.

Keogh, E. (1997), *Illicit Drug Use & Related Criminal Activity In The Dublin Metropolitan Area,* Research Report No. 8 / 98. Templemore, Co.Tipperary: Garda Research Unit.

Kessler, R.C. and W.J. McGee (1993), 'Childhood Adversities and Adult Depression: Basic Patterns of Association in a US National Study'. *Psychological Medicine,* 23:679-690.

Kiely, G. (2001) 'The Changing Role of Fathers' in Cleary, A., M. Nic Ghiolla Phádraig and S. Quin. (2001) *Understanding Children. Volume 2: Changing Experiences and Family Forms.* Dublin, Oak Tree Press.

Kimmel, M. S. (1987), 'Rethinking Masculinity: New Directions in Research' in: *Changing Men: New Directions in Research on Men and Masculinity.* Newbury Park, CA: Sage.

Kolvin, I., F.J.W. Miller, D.M. Scott, S.R.M. Gatzanie and M. Fleeting. (1990), *Continuities of Deprivation? The Newcastle 1000 Family Study.* Aldershot, UK: Avebury.

Lareau, A. (2000), 'Social Class and the Daily Lives of Children: a Study from the United States'. *Childhood*, 7:155-172.

Lawlor, M. and D. James. (2000), 'Prevalence of Psychological Problems in Irish School Going Adolescents'. *Irish Journal of Psychological Medicine*, 17:117-122.

Lazarus, R.S. and S. Folkman. (1984), *Stress, Appraisal and Coping.* New York: Springer Publishing Company.

Linehan, M.M., P. Camper, J.A. Chiles, K. Strosahl and E. Shearin. (1987), 'Interpersonal Problem Solving and Parasuicide'. *Cognitive Therapy Research*, 11(1): 1-12.

Lodge, A. and M. Flynn. (2001), 'Gender Identity in the Primary School Playground' in Cleary, A., M. Nic Ghiolla Phádraig and S. Quin. (2001) *Understanding Children. Volume 2: Changing Experiences and Family Forms.* Dublin: Oak Tree Press.

Loeber, R. (1990), 'Development and Risk Factors of Juvenile Antisocial Behaviour and Delinquency'. *Clinical Psychology Review*, 10: 1-41.

Lynch, K. (1998), 'The Status of Children and Young Persons: Educational and Related Issues' in: S. Healy and B. Reynolds (eds), *Social Policy in Ireland: Principles, Practice and Problems.* Dublin: Oak Tree Press.

Lynch, K. (1999), *Equality in Education*. Dublin: Gill and Macmillan.

Lynch, K., T. Brannick, P. Clancy and S. Drudy. (1999b), *Points and Performance in Higher Education: A Study of the Predictive Validity of the Points System*. Dublin: Government Publications.

Maccobe, E.E. and C.N. Jacklin (1974), *The Psychology of Sex Differences*. Stanford CA: Stanford University Press.

Mac an Ghaill (1996), 'What about the Boys? Schooling, Class and Crisis Masculinity'. *The Sociological Review*, 44 (3): 381-397.

Mac an Ghaill, M. (1994), *The Making of Men*. Buckingham: The Open University Press.

McCashin, A., (1996), *Lone Mothers in Ireland*. Dublin: Oak Tree Press/ Combat Poverty Agency.

McCullagh, C. (1991), 'A Tie That Binds: Family and Ideology in Ireland'. *Economic and Social Review*, 22: 199-212.

McCullagh, Ciaran. (1996) *Crime in Ireland : A Sociological Introduction*. Cork: Cork University Press.

McGivney, V. (1999), *Excluded Men: Men who are Missing Out from Education and Training*. Leicester UK: The National Organisation for Adult Learning.

MacInnes, J. (1998), *The End of Masculinity*. Buckingham: Open University Press.

McKeown, K., Ferguson, H. and Rooney, D. (2000), *Changing Fathers? Fatherhood and Family Life in Modern Ireland*. Cork: The Collins Press.

McMunn, A.,M. J. Y. Nazroo, M.G. Marmot, R. Boreham and R. Goodman. (2001), 'Children's Emotional and Behavioural Well-being and the Family Environment: Findings from the Health Survey for England'. *Social Science and Medicine*, 53:423-440.

Mayock, P. (2000), *Choosers or Losers: Influences on Young People's Choice about Drugs in Inner-city Dublin*. Dublin: Children's Research Centre, TCD.

Morgan, M. (1997) *International Adult Literacy Survey: Results for Ireland*. Dublin: Educational Research Centre.

National Economic and Social Forum (1997), *Early School Leavers and Youth Unemployment*, Forum Report No. 11. Dublin: NESF.

National Council for Curriculum and Assessment (NCCA) (1999), *From Junior to Leaving Certificate: A Longitudinal Study of 1994 Junior Certificate Candidates who took the Leaving Certificate Examination in 1997*. Dublin: Education Research Centre.

Nic Ghiolla Phádraig, M. (1992), 'Trends in Religious Practice in Ireland'. *Doctrine and Life*, 42 (1): 3-11.

Ní Laoire, C. (2001), 'A Matter of Life or Death? Men, Masculinities and Staying 'Behind' in Rural Ireland'. *Sociologia Ruralis, 41(2):220-236*.

Nolan, B. and Farrell, B. (1990), *Child Poverty in Ireland*. Dublin: Combat Poverty Agency.

Nolan, B. and Whelan, C.T. (1997), 'Unemployment and Health' in Cleary, A and Treacy, M. *The Sociology of Health and Illness in Ireland*, UCD Press: Dublin.

Nygaard Christoffersen, M. (2000), 'Growing Up with Unemployment: a Study of Parental Unemployment and Children's Risk of Abuse and Neglect Based on National Longitudinal 1973 Birth Cohorts in Denmark'. *Childhood*, 7 (4)

O'Brien, M., R. Moran, T. Kelleher and P. Cahill. (2000), *National Drug Treatment Reporting System, Statistical Bulletin 1997 and 1998*. Dublin: Health Research Board.

O'Brien, M. and R. Moran. (1998), *Overview of Drug Issues in Ireland 1997*. Dublin: Health Research Board.

O'Dwyer, K. (1998), *Juvenile Offending and the Juvenile Justice System in Ireland*, Research Report No.8/98. Templemore, Co. Tipperary: Garda Research Unit.

O'Mahony, P. (1997), *Mountjoy Prisoners: A Sociological and Criminological Profile*. Dublin: Department of Justice.

O'Mahony P. (1993), *Crime and Punishment in Ireland*. Dublin: Round Hall.

Ó Moráin, P. (1999), '*2,900 homeless adults in EHB area – survey.' Report on the Homeless Initiative study* . Irish Times 7th September, 1999.

Owens, T. (2000), *Men on the Move*. Dublin: Aontas.

Phillips, A. (1993), *The Trouble with Boys : Parenting the Men of the Future*. London: Pandora Press.

Rutter, M. (1979), 'Protective Factors in Children's Responses to Stress and Disadvantage' in M.W. Kent and J.E. Rolf (Eds.) *Primary Prevention of Psychopathology, Vol.3: Social Competence of children*. Hanover, NH: University Press of New England.

Rutter, M. (1987), 'Psychological Resilience and Protective Mechanisms.'. *American Journal of Orthopsychiatry*, 57: 316-331.

Rutter, M. (1989), 'Pathways from Childhood to Adult Life'. *Journal of Child Psychology and Psychiatry*, 30l: 23-51.

Rutter, M. and D. Quinton. (1977), 'Psychiatric Disorders: Ecological Factors and Concepts of Causation' in H. McGurk (Ed.) *Education, Health and Behaviour*. London: Longman.

Rutter, M. and D.J. Smith. (1995), *Psychosocial Disorders in Young People: Time Trends and Their Causes*. Chichester: Wiley for Academia Europaea.

Rutter, M. H. Giller, and A. Hagell. (1998), *Anti-social Behaviour by Young People*. Cambridge, UK: Cambridge University Press.

146

Scheper-Hughes, N. (1979), *Saints, Scholars and Schizophrenics: Mental Illness in Ireland*. London: University of California Press.

Sheerin, D., Maguire, R. and Robinson, J. (1999), ' A 15-month Follow-up Study of Children Admitted to a Child Psychiatric Inpatient Unit'. *Irish Journal of Psychological Medicine*, 16, 97-103.

Smith, J., Gilford, S. and O'Sullivan, A. (1998), *The Family Background of Homeless Young People*. London: Family Policy Studies Centre.

Smyth, E. (1997) 'Labour Market Structures and Women's Employment in the Republic of Ireland' in Berne, A. and M. Leonard. *Women and Irish Society*. Belfast: Beyond the Pale Publications.

Stack, S. (1998), 'The Relationship of Female Labor Force Participation to Suicide: a Comparative Analysis'. *Archives of Suicide Research* 4: 249-261.

Stack, S. (1987) *Suicide: A Comparative Analysis*, Social Forces, 57, 644-653.

Stack. S. (2000a), 'Suicide: A 15-year Review of the Sociological Literature, Part 1: Cultural and Economic Factors'. *Suicide and Life-Threatening Behaviour*, 30(2) 145-162.

Swinburne, B. (1999), *Unmarried Lone Parents on Welfare: A Changing Profile?*, Unpublished dissertation. Institute of Public Administration, Dublin.

Tuohy, D. (2002), 'Youth 2K: The Multiple Worlds of Young People' in Cassidy, E.G. *Measuring Ireland: Discerning Values and Beliefs*. Dublin: Veritas Publications.

Veenhoven, R. (1999), 'Quality of Life in Individualistic Society'. *Social Indicators Research*, 48: 157-186.

Wasserman, I. (1990) 'A Longitudinal Study of the Linkage between Divorce and Suicide, Family Perspective', 24: 61-67.

Webster, D. (1997a), 'Promoting Jobs Could Reduce Lone Parenthood', *Working Brief*, October: 20-22.

Whelan, C.T., Layte, R., Maitre, B., Gannon, B., Nolan, B., Watson, D. and Williams, J. (2003) *Monitoring Poverty Trends in Ireland: Results from the 2001 Living in Ireland Survey*. Policy Research Series 51. Dublin: Economic and Social Research Institute.

White (1990), 'Determinants of Divorce: A Review of Research in the Eighties'. *Journal of Marriage and the Family*, 52: 904-912.

Williams, J. and M. O'Connor (1999), *Counted In, The Report of the 1999 Assessment of Homeless in Dublin, Kildare and Wicklow*. Dublin: Economic and Social Research Institute.

Willis, P. (1977), *Learning to Labour: How Working Class Kids Get Working Class Jobs*. Fernborough UK: Saxon House.